Scroll Saw Fretwork Patterns

Patrick Spielman & James Reidle

Drawings by
Dirk Boelman,
The Art Factory

 Sterling Publishing Co., Inc.   New York

Edited by Laurel Ornitz

Library of Congress Cataloging-in-Publication Data

Spielman, Patrick.
  Scroll saw fretwork patterns.

  Includes index.
  1. Fretwork—Themes, motives. I. Reidle, James.
II. Title.
NK9930.S8 1989   684′.08   88-30813
ISBN 0-8069-6998-9

  5 7 9 10 8 6 4

Copyright © 1989 by Patrick Spielman and James Reidle
Published by Sterling Publishing Co., Inc.
387 Park Avenue South, New York, N.Y. 10016
Distributed in Canada by Sterling Publishing
℅ Canadian Manda Group, P.O. Box 920, Station U
Toronto, Ontario, Canada M8Z 5P9
Distributed in Great Britain and Europe by Cassell PLC
Artillery House, Artillery Row, London SW1P 1RT, England
Distributed in Australia by Capricorn Ltd.
P.O. Box 665, Lane Cove, NSW 2066
Manufactured in the United States of America

Contents

ACKNOWLEDGMENTS   *5*

INTRODUCTION   *6*

Patterns

Silhouettes   *14*

Country Designs   *29*

Home Accessories   *36*

Mirror & Photo Frames   *54*

Musical Designs   *65*

Birds   *68*

Animals   *88*

Alphabets & Numbers   *102*

Signs   *114*

Shelves   *138*

Delicate Brackets   *172*

Architectural Brackets   *179*

Balusters   *184*

Running Trim   *186*

Victorian Arches   *190*

Gable Ornaments   *195*

Grilles *198*

Inlays & Overlays *203*

Christmas Ornaments *209*

Arrows *211*

Nautical Silhouettes *212*

Wheels *216*

Vehicles *218*

Miniatures *224*

Clocks *227*

Miscellaneous Patterns *245*

METRIC EQUIVALENCY CHART *250*

ABOUT THE AUTHORS *251*

CURRENT BOOKS BY PATRICK SPIELMAN *252*

INDEX *255*

Acknowledgments

We are especially grateful to our good woodworking friends who have contributed to the content and the overall impact of this book. Their generosity in sharing plans and ideas to help spread and improve the art and craft of scroll-saw fretwork has been very gratifying.

First, and most importantly, we extend thanks to Henry Aldinger for contributing pattern sources and other historical material. We appreciate his dedicated efforts, which have evolved into a major part of the book.

We want to thank our friend and master fretworker, Carl Weckhorst, for sharing so many fretwork patterns and ideas. Carl and his wife, Phyllis, allowed us to photograph several of his extraordinary fretwork pieces in their home for this book.

Likewise, Kirk Ratajesak, also known as "the fretworker," has generously donated many of his original miniature designs and other patterns, which, along with the photographs of his work, also fill a number of these pages.

Many great patterns and some completed pieces that we captured with the camera were enthusiastically provided by talented fretsawer John Polhemus of J.P. Woodworks, Waldorf, Maryland. Some of his patterns are sure to become woodworking classics, and we are certainly happy to include them here.

We also want to thank Hanns Derke of Advanced Machinery Imports, Ltd. for allowing us to adapt two patterns from AMI's pattern book to include in ours. In addition, we want to thank Don Strong of Strong Tool Design, who helped us with leads and suggestions.

The skillful rendering of the patterns by Dirk Boelman of the Art Factory, Richland Center, Wisconsin, is a very special feature of this book. We are grateful to Dirk Boelman not only for his graphic arts talent, but also for his patience, understanding, and steadfast dedication—and for the friendship that developed while we were working on the book.

Others who in one way or another influenced the outcome of this book include Elaine Reidle and Patricia Spielman, Mark Obernberger, Larry Boehner, Conrad Jensen, Ken Gould, and Gus Stefureac—to all, we express our appreciation for helping us bring *Scroll Saw Fretwork Patterns* to all woodworkers.

Patrick Spielman, Spielmans Wood Works, and
James Reidle, Reidle Products

Introduction

This book offers numerous full-size fretwork patterns for scroll sawing. Fretwork objects generally are more ornate and delicate, and have substantially more piercing cuts, or cutout open spaces, than other scroll-sawn objects. Still, doing fretwork can be great fun for everyone—male or female, from age 8 to 80.

Fretwork is really nothing new. In fact, fretwork was the national woodworking craze in the United States as far back as the early 1800s, and its popularity continued into the 1940s. Furthermore, historical records indicate that fretwork flourished in many other countries—including England, France, Italy, Switzerland, Germany, and Spain—perhaps centuries before it became the woodworking rage it did in the United States.

The essential difference between 18th-century and 19th-century fretwork has to do with the tools that were used. Much of the early fretwork made abroad was cut with hand-held saw frames that look and function like the hand-held coping saws of today. During the mid- to late 1800s, foot-powered scroll saws—the forerunners of our modern constant-tension parallel-arm scroll saws—were developed in the United

States, and this brought about abrupt changes in fretwork. With the foot-powered scroll saws came increased production output, accuracy, and speed, making fretwork easier and even more enjoyable.

During the 1800s scroll-sawing fretwork projects was often a family activity, for rich and poor alike. Back then, leisure time fretwork took the place of TV, videos, and other kinds of family entertainment. In some circles, fretwork was even considered a serious art form. Others involved with fretwork were employed in industry. They produced the Victorian gingerbread architectural embellishments that were so popular around the turn of the century.

This book provides many patterns that were popular over a century ago as well as other patterns that represent more contemporary design trends. However, all the patterns in the book are sawn by using the same essential techniques, which are fairly easy to master.

The interest in fretwork now appears to be resurfacing once again, and vigorously at that. This has no doubt been spurred on by the current resurgence of scroll sawing in general, which is probably due to the introduction of the modern constant-tension scroll saws during the late 1970s and early 1980s. Today there is a wide range of excellent tools and scroll-sawing machines, which makes scroll sawing and fretwork easier and more fun than ever before in history. Consequently, and perhaps for the exact same reasons it was so popular some centuries ago, fretwork is about to emerge again as a major woodworking activity. Here are some reasons why fretwork is so popular:

- Fretwork is a useful spare time activity.
- It requires very little space.
- The tools and materials required are relatively inexpensive.

- You can fit fretwork into a busy schedule, starting and stopping whenever it's convenient.
- Fretsawing provides an immediate sense of achievement and accomplishment.
- Fret projects can be as simple or complex as you desire.
- Fretwork is a good activity for all ages and all woodworking levels.
- New project ideas, plans, and patterns, as well as improved tools, are introduced regularly to freshen and inspire the overall state of the art.

Patterns—Copying, Enlarging or Reducing, and Transferring

Naturally, we feel we have developed and provided you with patterns that are appropriate in terms of style and size. However, we realize that special individual needs may arise causing some patterns to require certain alterations. Thus, we encourage you to make size enlargements or reductions as well as design modifications to suit your individual needs.

You can change pattern sizes in a number of different ways. The most mod-

Illus. 1. An office copy machine is ideal for reproducing patterns from this book, and some machines also have the capability to enlarge or reduce, as shown.

ern and popular approach is to use a copy machine. Patterns can not only be copied in a one to one size scale, but they can also be enlarged or reduced to any size simply with the touch of a button. See Illus. 1.

Other conventional enlargement or reduction procedures are the use of a pantograph and the graph square, or grid, method. A pantograph is an inexpensive tool that can be used to enlarge a pattern as much as ten times its original size or reduce it down to one tenth of its original size. The enlargement or reduction can be drawn directly onto the workpiece or onto paper.

To enlarge a pattern with the grid method, begin with some transparent tissue paper. Accurately rule it out, making a grid of ¼″ or ½″ squares. Placing the tissue paper over the pattern, trace the lines of the design. Next, on a larger piece of paper, about the size that you want the eventual pattern to be, divide the space up with exactly the same number of squares. The size of the larger set of squares can also be determined by the enlargement ratio desired. If you want the design twice the original size, then draw the large squares twice the size of the smaller ones. Now, copy the design square by square onto the larger grid. Curves may be drawn by eye after you've located them with reference to their surrounding square; however, it is more accurate to mark the points where the line of the curve strikes each horizontal and vertical line. To reduce a pattern, follow this procedure in reverse.

With this technique, you can also draw the design directly on the surface of the wood. However, usually the pattern is drawn onto paper first since it's easier to erase, refine, and smooth out contoured lines on paper. When you've made your full-size paper pattern, you have several choices of how to transfer the pattern to the wood.

The method that we recommend involves the use of special spray adhesives (Illus. 2) that temporarily bond paper copies of patterns to the workpiece surfaces. Bonding copy-machine copies of patterns to the wood is the easiest and quickest method that we know of or have tested.

Another way to transfer patterns to wood involves tracing the pattern from the book and then transferring this pattern to the workpiece with carbon or graphite paper. Incidentally, graphite paper is preferable to carbon paper. Since carbon paper is greasy, it's hard to erase from wood, and any remaining marks left on the surface are very difficult to finish over. Graphite paper, on the other hand, erases easily and sands away without difficulty, and it's also available in white as well as dark. White graphite paper is ideal for transferring patterns to darker woods, such as walnut, cherry, and padauk. See Illus. 3. Graphite paper is

Illus. 2. These spray adhesives are perfect for bonding copies of patterns directly to the wood. The pattern and the wood are then cut together.

available at most office-supply and graphic arts stores.

The use of a pattern template (Illus. 4) is still another way of transferring patterns to wood surfaces. A template is nothing more than a full-size pattern made of stiff, rigid material that can be easily traced around. Templates can be cut from a variety of different materials with a scissors or knife, but the easiest way to make them is to saw them out when you saw the basic shape of the project. Suitable template materials include tagboard, cardboard, file folder stock, oiled stencil board, and thin plastics. Unlike pasted-down patterns, which get cut up during the sawing, you can reuse good templates again and again.

Wood Materials

In the pre-plywood days some decades ago, only solid woods were used for fretwork projects since they were the only wood materials available. Although most serious fretworkers and masters of the art today prefer using solid woods, you shouldn't overlook the many advantages and conveniences afforded by conventional plywood

Illus. 3. Graphite paper works better than carbon paper for transferring designs, and it's available in white for use on dark woods.

Illus. 4. Cardboard templates can be used, as shown, to transfer the pattern to the wood. Templates can be reused again and again.

and other modern materials. Even though the edges of fret-sawn plywoods are obviously less desirable than those of solid woods for some applications and are frequently more difficult to finish and conceal, plywoods offer more strength and durability than many of the solid materials. Plywoods are good for very fragile and delicate cuttings; and since they are available in large lengths and widths, in thin thicknesses, they are ideal for large patterns and projects. See Illus. 5.

Most traditional fretwork is cut from material that is ¼", or less, thick, which makes plywood appear to be the logical choice for many projects. However, the smaller projects tend to be better-looking while also fairly sturdy when sawn from quality thin solid woods. Today, many woodworkers have small planers in their home shops for preparing their own material (Illus. 6). If you don't have your own planer, you can purchase small quantities of thin, solid, fancy woods, in ⅛", ¼", and ½" thicknesses by mail order. Fine hardwood plywoods—such as teak, cherry, walnut, mahogany, zebra, and maple—as well as micro lumber in standard or exotic species can be obtained from some major outlets.

Illus. 5. You can use thin hardwood plywoods of any species for fretwork projects.

Illus. 6. Thin solid woods are ideal for many fret projects— but especially for those where the edges of the plywoods may be objection- able. Small shop planers, such as the one shown here, can reduce your stock to any thickness desired.

The Basics and Getting Started

The entire process of fretwork revolves around the technique of making inside cutouts of various designs. This is known as piercing work. See Illus. 7 and 8. The process is very straightforward: First, you drill holes into the waste, or areas that will be cut away. Next, you thread the blade through, reclamp and retension the blade in the saw, and then proceed to complete the cutout. You repeat this process as many times as necessary to finish the project.

If you are a beginner, it's best to start with the less complex pieces, avoiding designs that require numerous cutouts and those that have very distinct repetitive shapes within themselves. Ornate designs with identical geometrical forms on either side as well as very delicate large pieces should not be undertaken until you've gained some experience. However, skill at working the saw and material together in harmony will come quickly and automatically with little conscious effort. For your first few projects, select patterns that you can complete within a short work period. In the course of working these smaller projects, you will be able to get a good idea of how much work you can do within a given time period. If you start with a very complex or highly ornate design that requires much more time than you initially may want to invest, you are likely to rush and make mistakes. So, start with short projects and allow yourself to enjoy the pleasurable and rewarding craft fretwork is intended to be.

As you work through this book, you will come across some special techniques that will enhance your work. One helpful technique is stack cutting, which refers to cutting multiple pieces of the same design, one on top of the other, all at once. See Illus. 9. Not only does this method increase output but it also guarantees that all resulting pieces will be absolutely identical.

Illus. 7. Inside openings are made by drilling holes in the area that is to be cut away; then the blade can be threaded through the work-piece and reclamped.

Illus. 8. A typical cutting job in progress.

11

Illus. 9. Cutting several layers of stock at once is called stack cutting. Note how easily the pattern, temporarily bonded to the wood with a special spray adhesive, is removed.

Multiple Uses of Patterns

Many of the patterns in this book can be used as ornamental features, as is. They can be used as inlays, overlays, and other types of decorative embellishments on boxes, cabinet doors, furniture, and architectural panels. The book provides patterns for various alphabets, signs, country designs, Christmas items, silhouettes, shelves, picture frames, and projects in many other categories—which can be combined and interchanged, creating a variety of new uses. You should also be aware of the designs that are possible by using only certain segments of a particular design motif. For example, with the pattern shown in Illus. 71 on pages 84–85, you can lift the hummingbird from the flower and frame design. Or, you can simply use the pattern for the outer frame, eliminating the floral and hummingbird interior. In addition, many patterns can be revised by omitting some of the cutout spaces, thereby making the project less complicated and quicker to complete. Being aware of these multiple usages should help you get the most from the patterns provided here.

Patterns

Silhouettes

Illus. 10. Cupid silhouette pattern.

Illus. 11. Tree, apple, flower, and sailboat silhouette patterns.

Illus. 12. Unicorn silhouette pattern.

Illus. 13. Old-fashioned bicyclist silhouette pattern.

Illus. 14. Seated-girl silhouette, designed and sawn by John Polhemus. (Turn to pages 20—21 for the pattern.)

Illus. 15. A closeup look at the line-work detailing achieved by the saw kerf. The white and black lines are all saw cuts; the black lines are simply shaded by the angle of the camera lens.

Illus. 16. Family supper silhouette. (Turn to pages 22–23 for the pattern.)

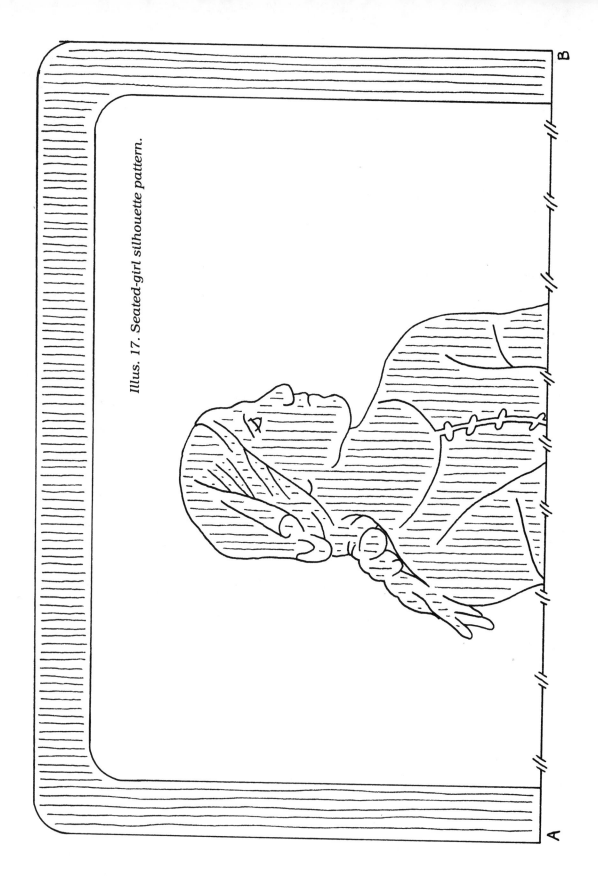

Illus. 17. Seated-girl silhouette pattern.

20

21

A

B

Illus. 18. Family supper silhouette pattern.

A

B

23

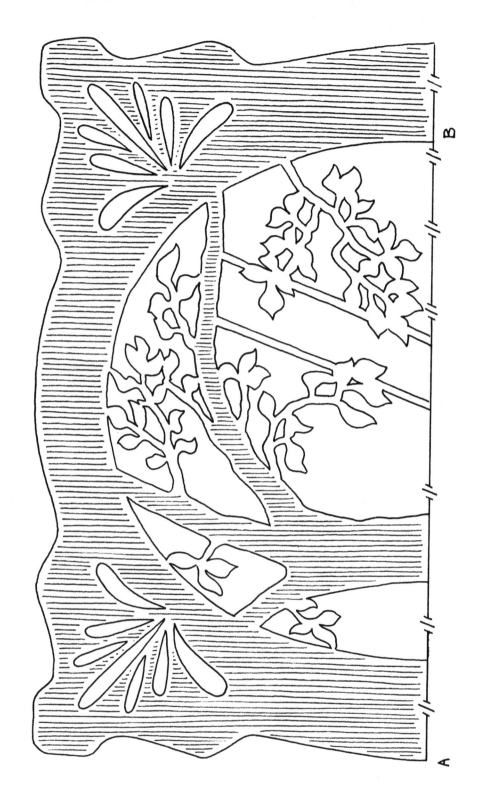

Illus. 19. Girl-in-swing silhouette pattern.

24

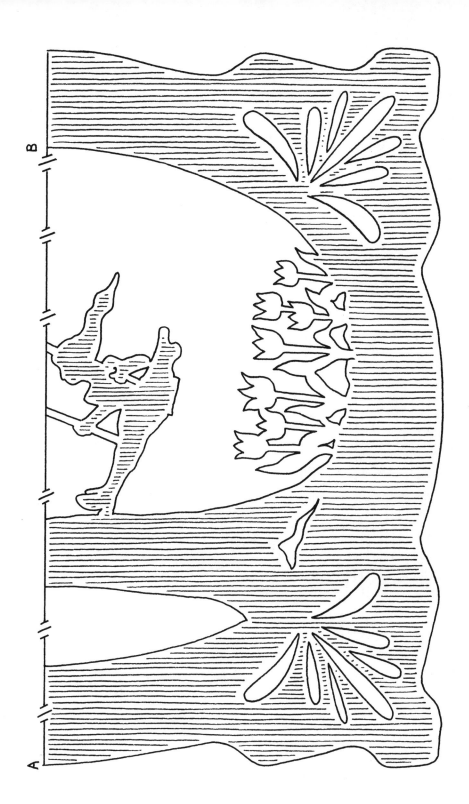

B

A

A

B

Illus. 20. Horse-and-carriage silhouette pattern.

A

B

27

Illus. 21. Woman's portrait silhouette pattern.

Country Designs

Illus. 22. Heart-shaped wreath pattern.

Illus. 23. Pineapple pattern.

Illus. 24. Lamp pattern.

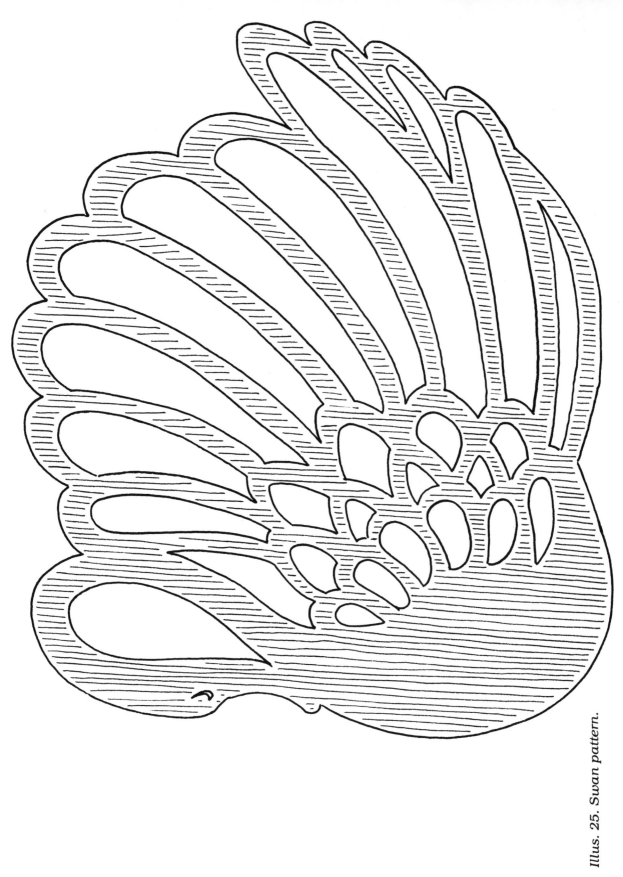

Illus. 25. Swan pattern.

Illus. 26. Swan pattern.

Illus. 27. Butterfly pattern.

Illus. 28. Welcome-sign pattern.

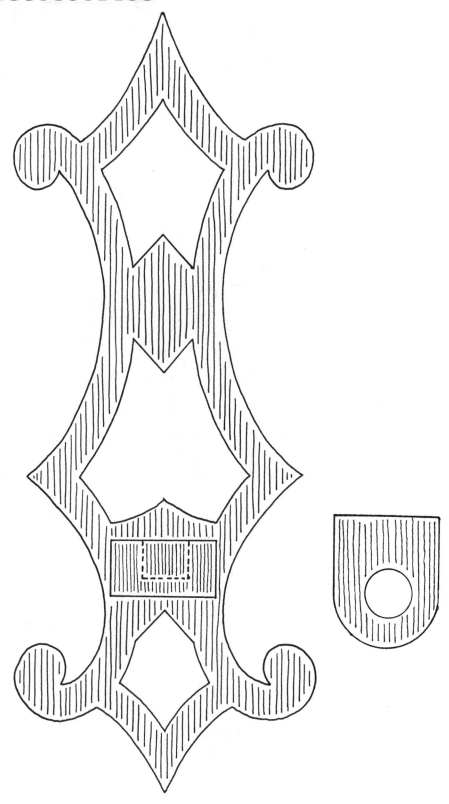

Illus. 29. Candle-holder pattern.

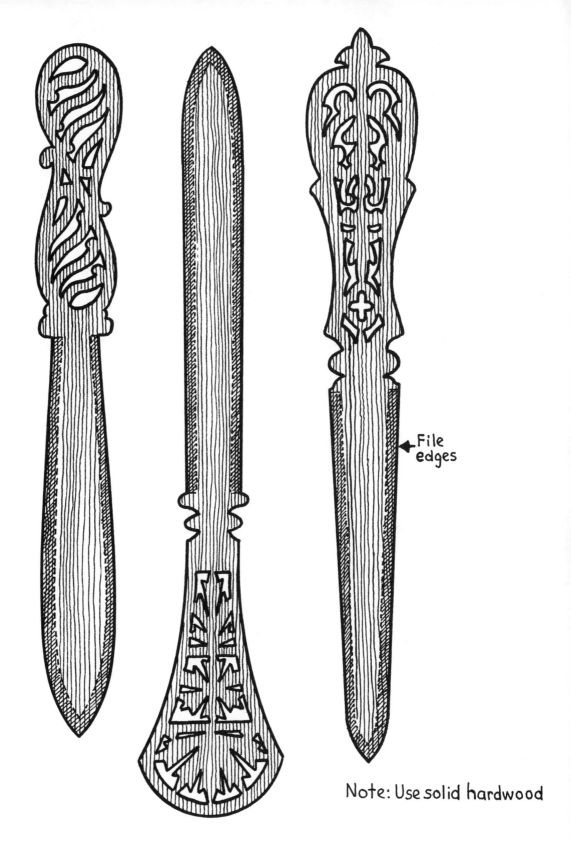

File edges

Note: Use solid hardwood

Illus. 30. Letter-opener patterns.

Illus. 31. Plant-hanger pattern. (Continued on the next page.)

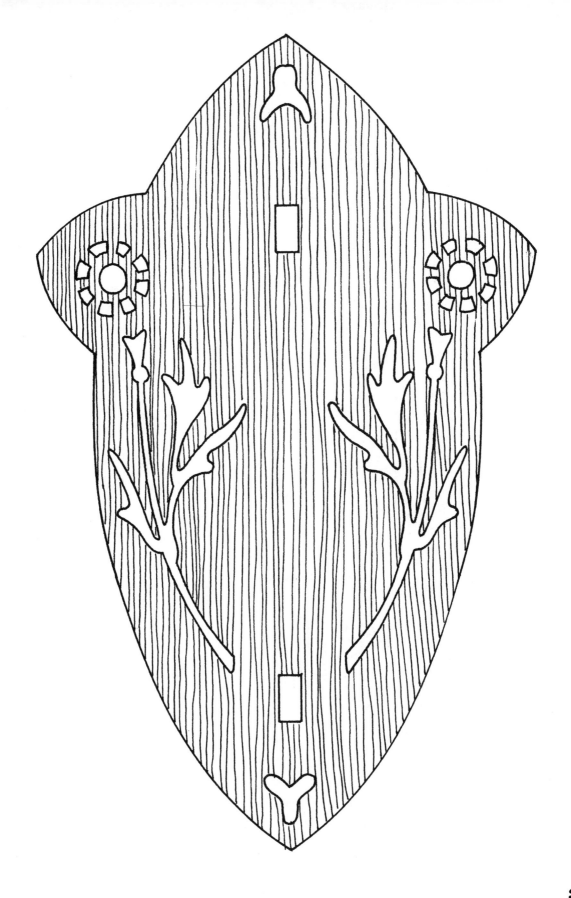

A   B

Illus. 32. Hand-mirror pattern. The pattern on the opposite page is overlaid on the larger pattern above to form a rabbet to receive the mirror.

40

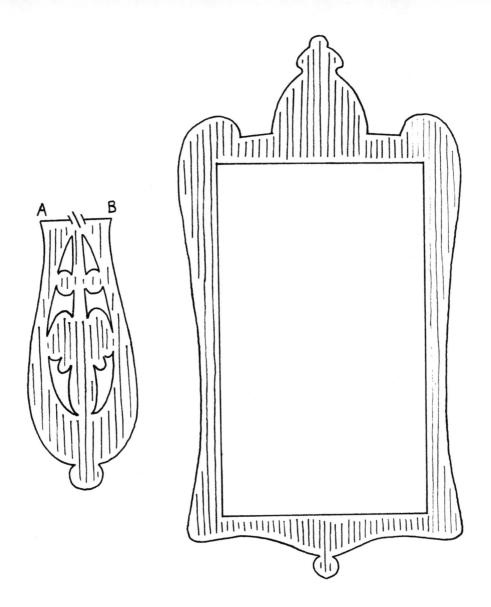

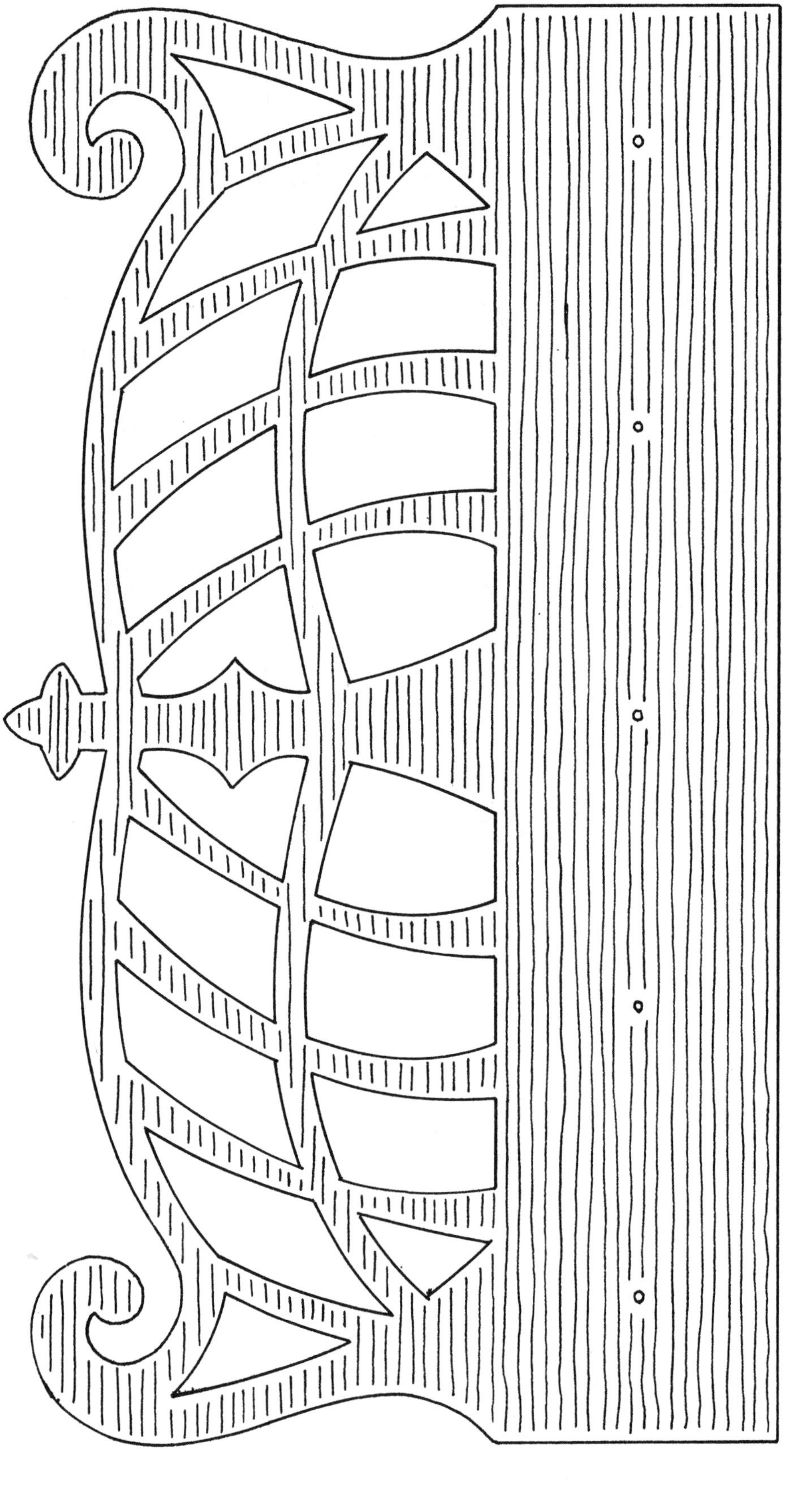

Illus. 33. Key-rack pattern.

Illus. 34. Pencil holder, by Henry Aldinger. (The pattern follows.)

Illus. 35. Pencil-holder pattern.

Illus. 36. Wheelbarrow, made of ³⁄₁₆″ walnut. (The pattern follows.)

45

Illus. 37. Wheelbarrow pattern (continued on the next page).
Use ¼" dowel axle and drill a ¼" hole in the wheel.

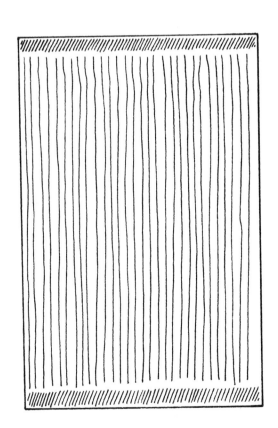

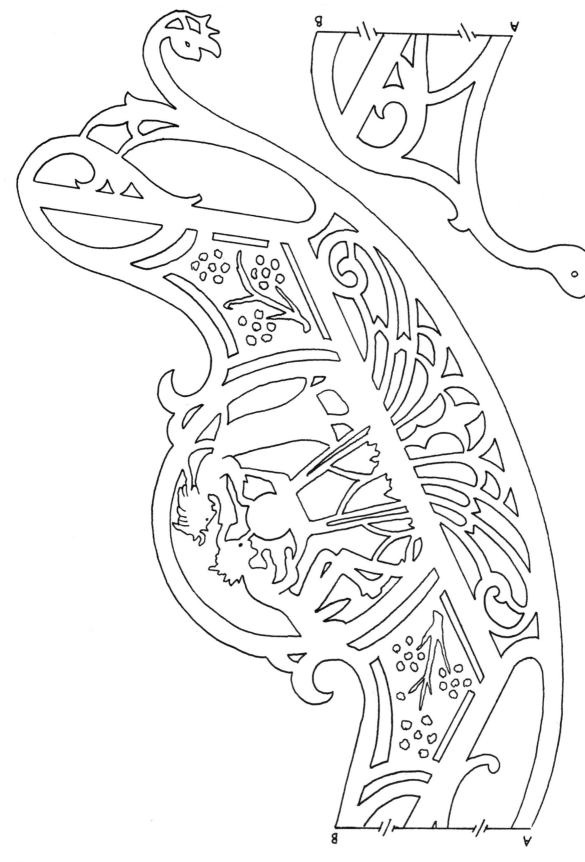

Illus. 38. Card-holder pattern. (Continued on the next page.)

(2 Pieces)

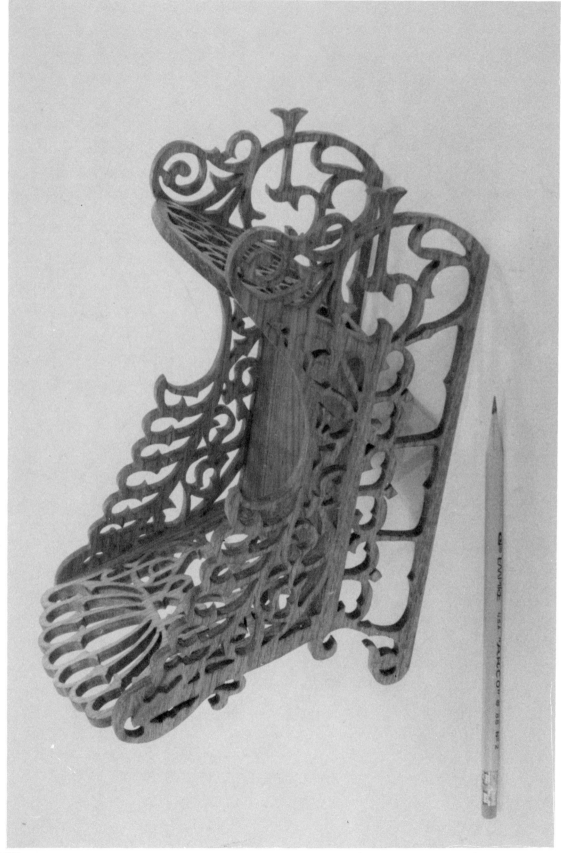

Illus. 39. Sleigh.

Illus. 40. Sleigh pattern. (Continued on the next two pages.)

B
A

B   A

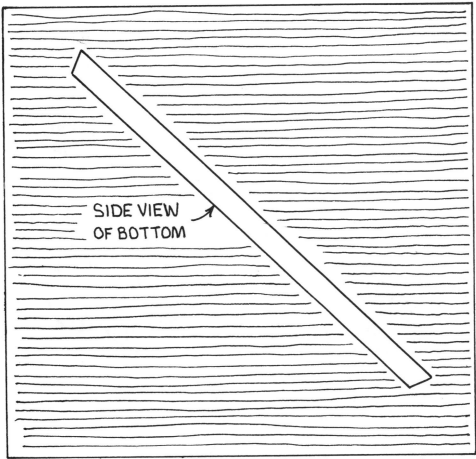

SIDE VIEW
OF BOTTOM

Mirror & Photo Frames

Illus. 41. Pattern for oval frame. Design by Kirk Ratajesak.

Illus. 42. Pattern for heart-shaped frame. Design by Kirk Ratajesak.

Illus. 43. Pattern for rectangular picture frame. Design by Dirk Boelman.

Illus. 44. Pattern for rectangular frame.
Design by Kirk Ratajesak.

Illus. 45. Rectangular and square frame designs, by Kirk Ratajesak. (The patterns follow.)

Illus. 46 (left). Strips that are ⅛" × ½" and overlaid make the rabbet for the photo or mirror. Illus. 47 (right). The rear of the frame showing the rabbet.

Illus. 48. Pattern for square frame.

Illus. 49. Pattern for rectangular frame.

Illus. 50. Rectangular frame design, by Kirk Ratajesak.

Illus. 51. Pattern for rectangular frame.

Illus. 52. Pattern for mirror frame with shelf.

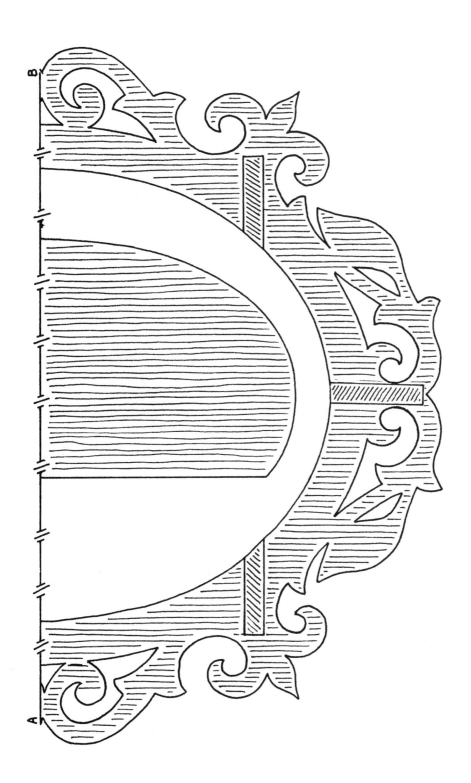

Illus. 53. Pattern for standing photo frame.

64

Musical Designs

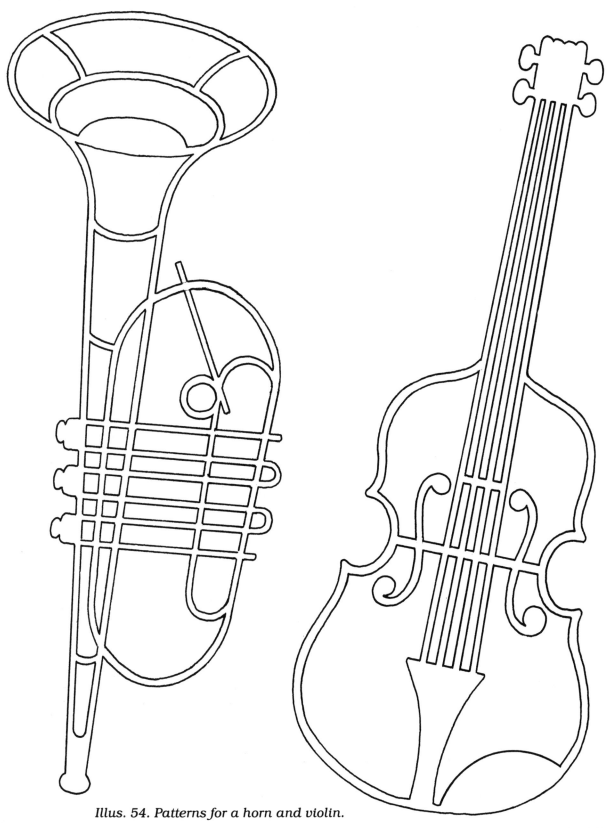

Illus. 54. Patterns for a horn and violin.

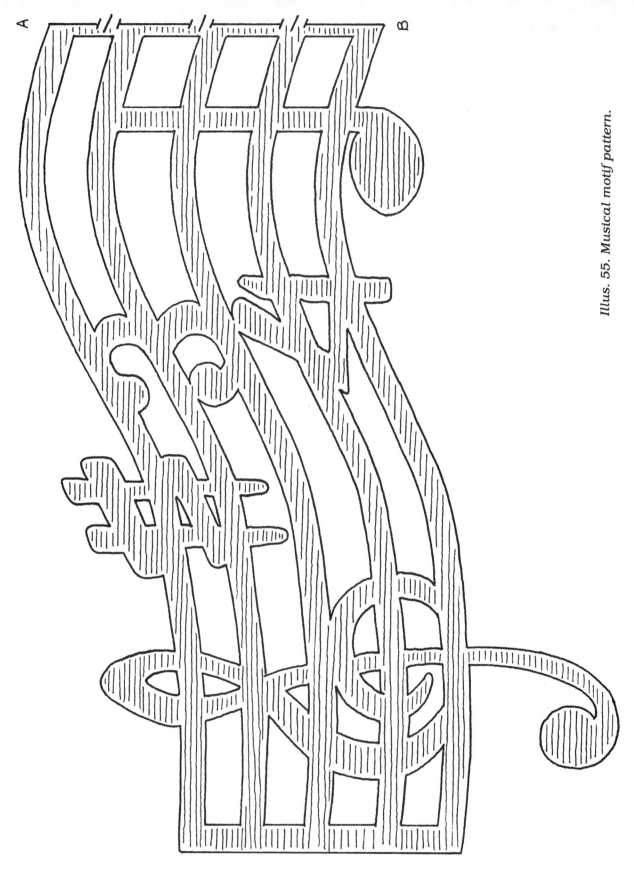

Illus. 55. Musical motif pattern.

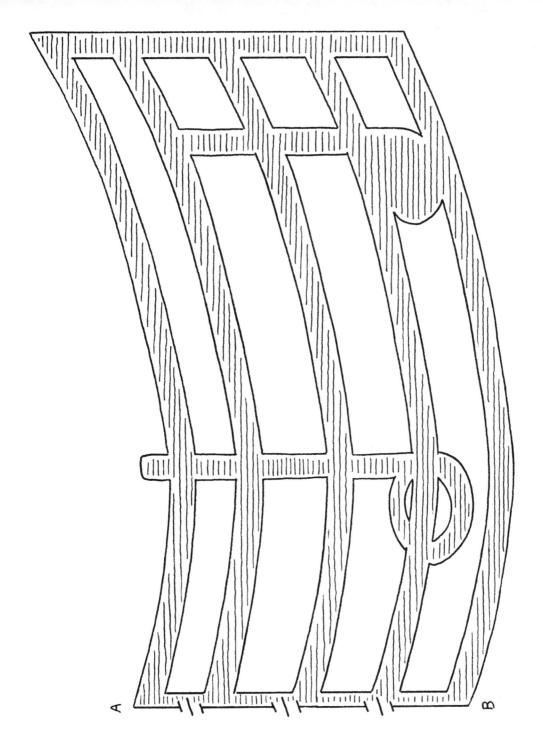

Birds

Illus. 56. Bird patterns.

Illus. 57. Bird patterns.

Illus. 58. Bird pattern.

Illus. 59. Birds pattern.

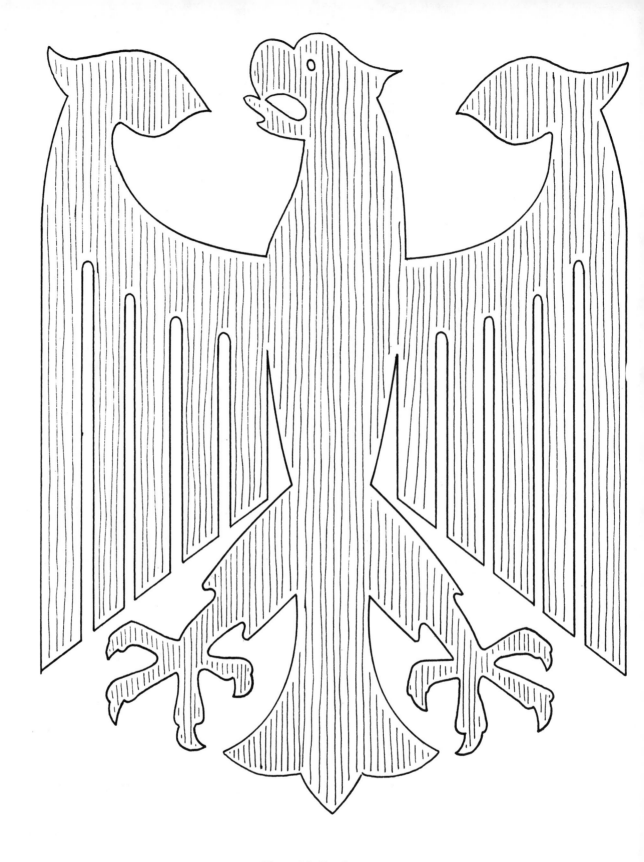

Illus. 60. Bird pattern.

Illus. 61. Stork design.

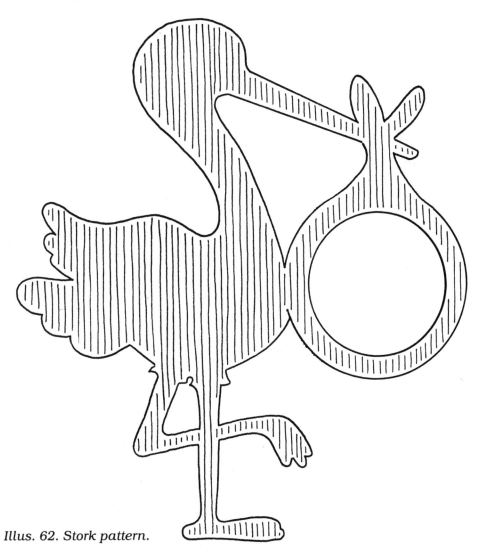

Illus. 62. Stork pattern.

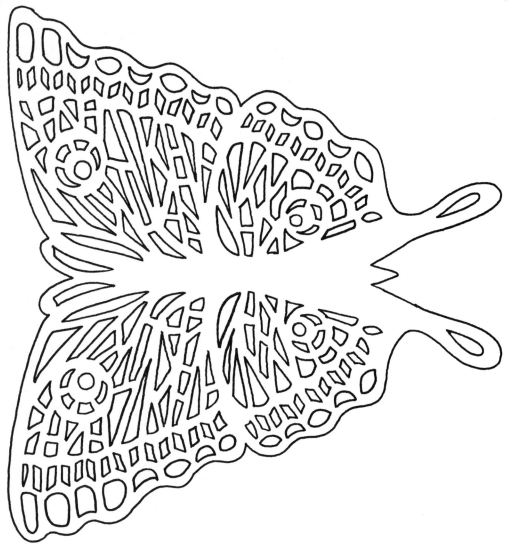

Illus. 63. Bird and butterfly patterns.

Illus. 64. Bird patterns.

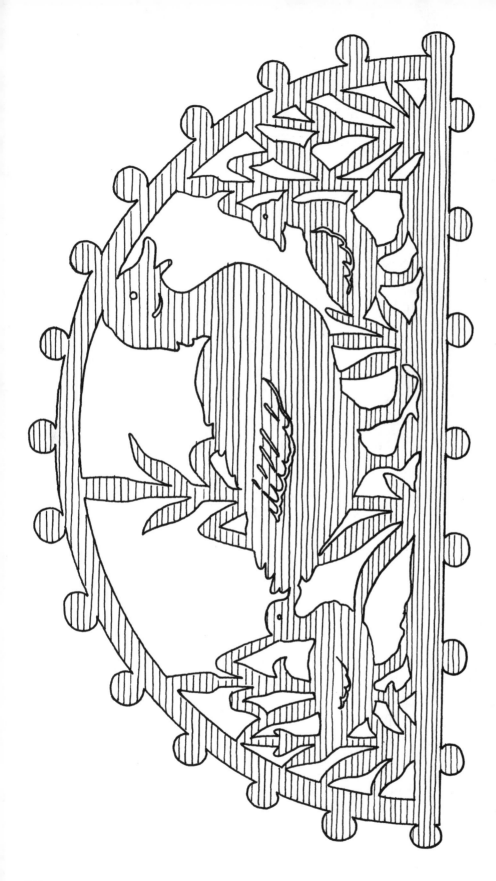

Illus. 65. Birds pattern.

Illus. 66. Bird pattern.

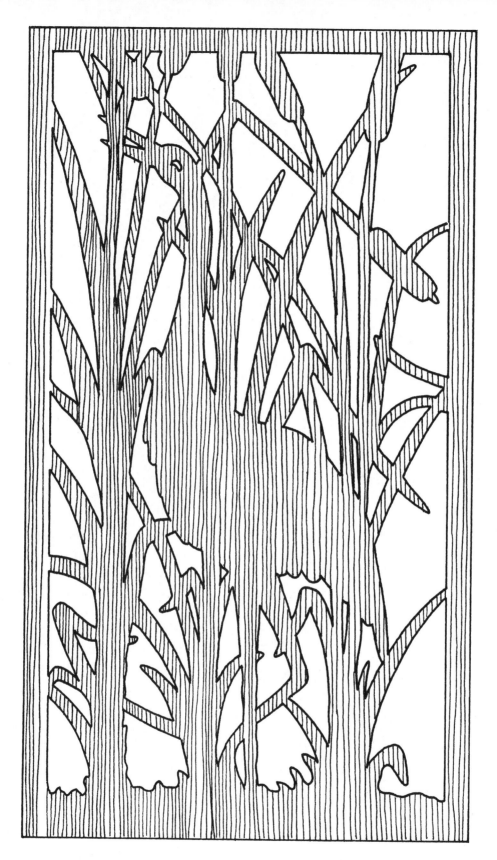

Illus. 67. Bird pattern.

Illus. 68. Ducks. (The patterns follow.)

A

B

Illus. 69. Duck pattern.

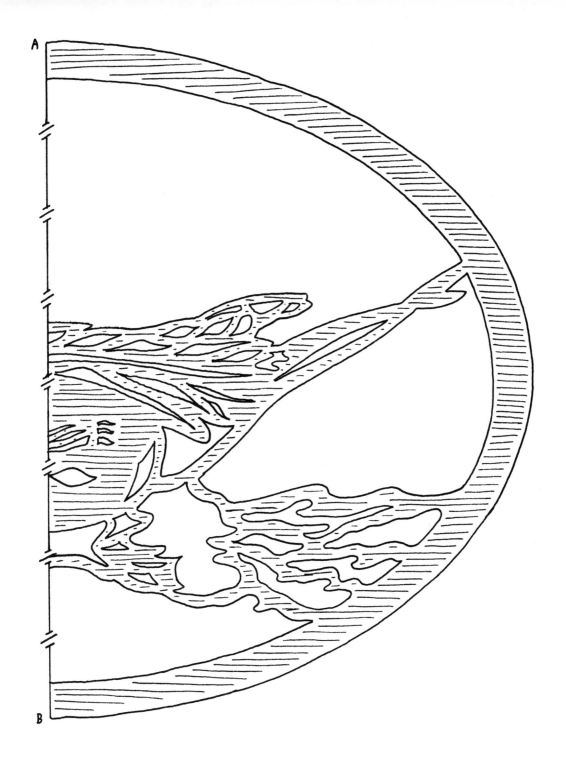

A

B

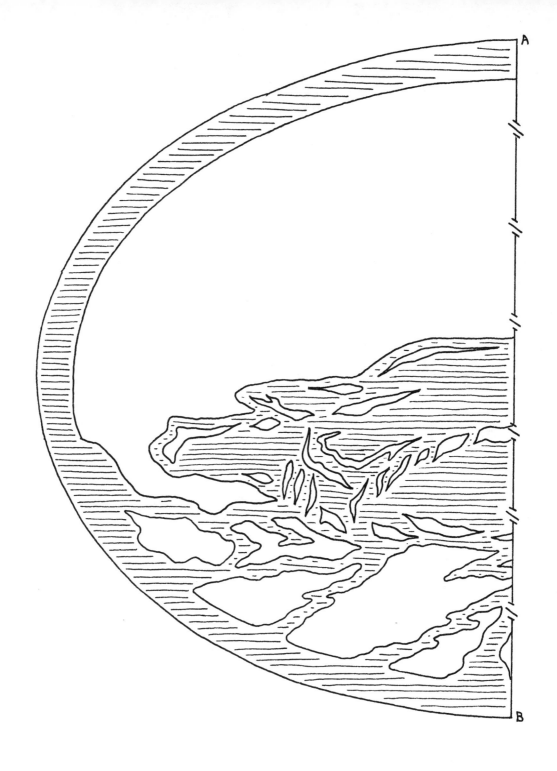

Illus. 70. Duck pattern.

83

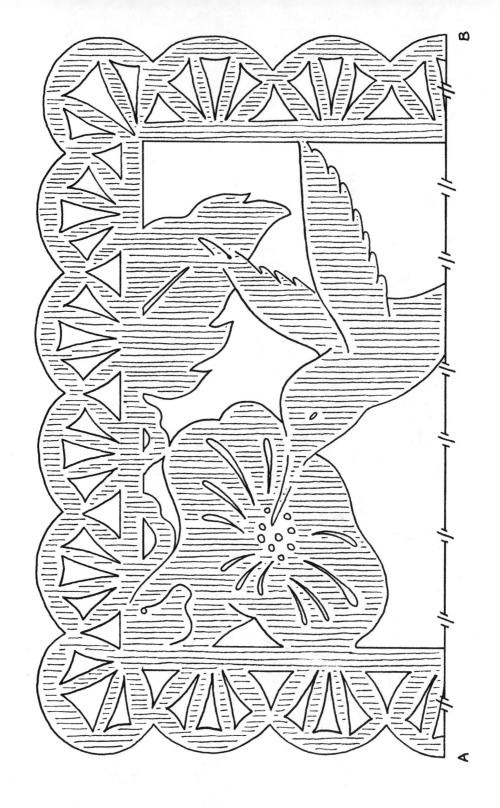

Illus. 71. Hummingbird pattern.

84

Illus. 72. Roosters pattern.

Illus. 73. Owl and bat pattern.

Animals

Illus. 74. Deer pattern.

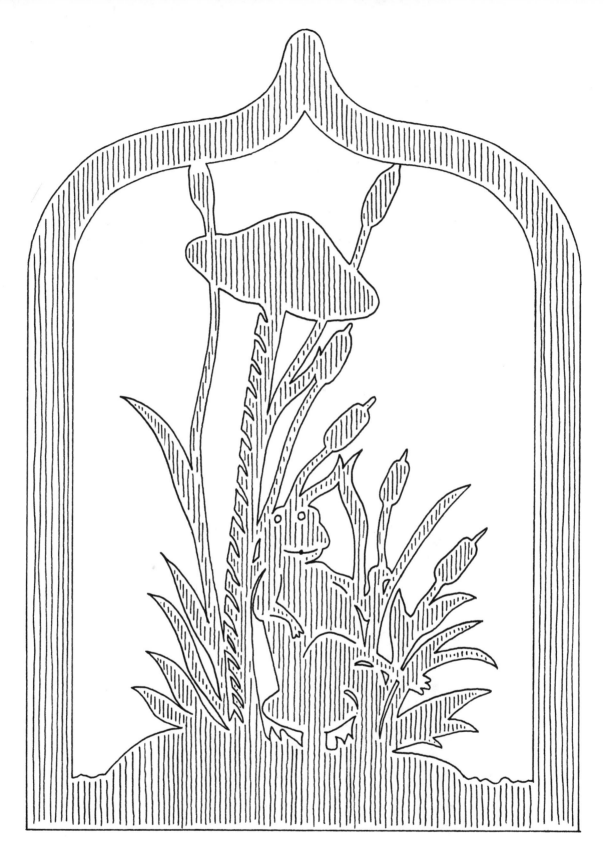

Illus. 75. Frog pattern.

Illus. 76. Cat pattern.

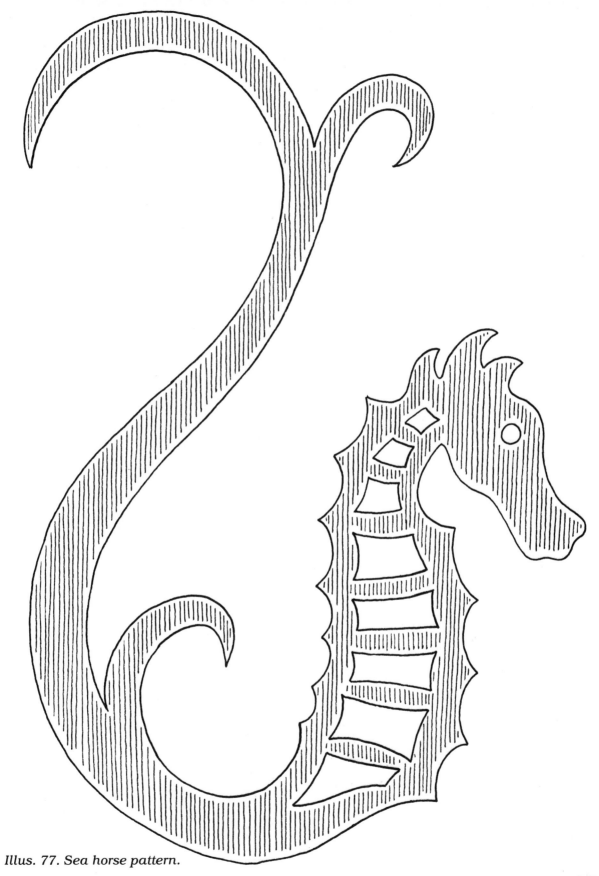

Illus. 77. Sea horse pattern.

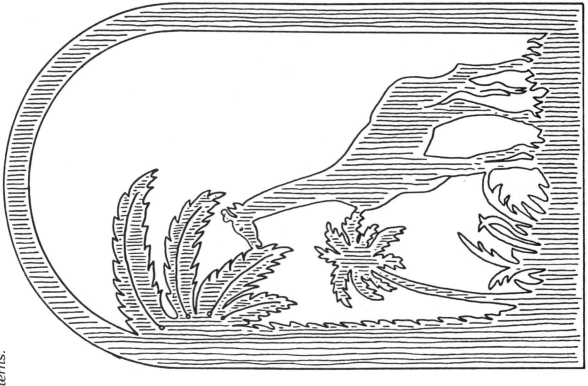

Illus. 79. Horse pattern.

Illus. 80. Deer pattern.

Illus. 81. This design, crafted by John Polhemus, is sawn from ¼" mahogany and placed on a black velvet background. (The pattern appears on the following pages.)

Illus. 82. Here is the dragon framed under glass.

A

B

Illus. 83. Dragon pattern.

A

B

97

Illus. 84. Griffin pattern.

Illus. 85. Unicorns, designed by Kirk Ratajesak

Illus. 86. Unicorn pattern.

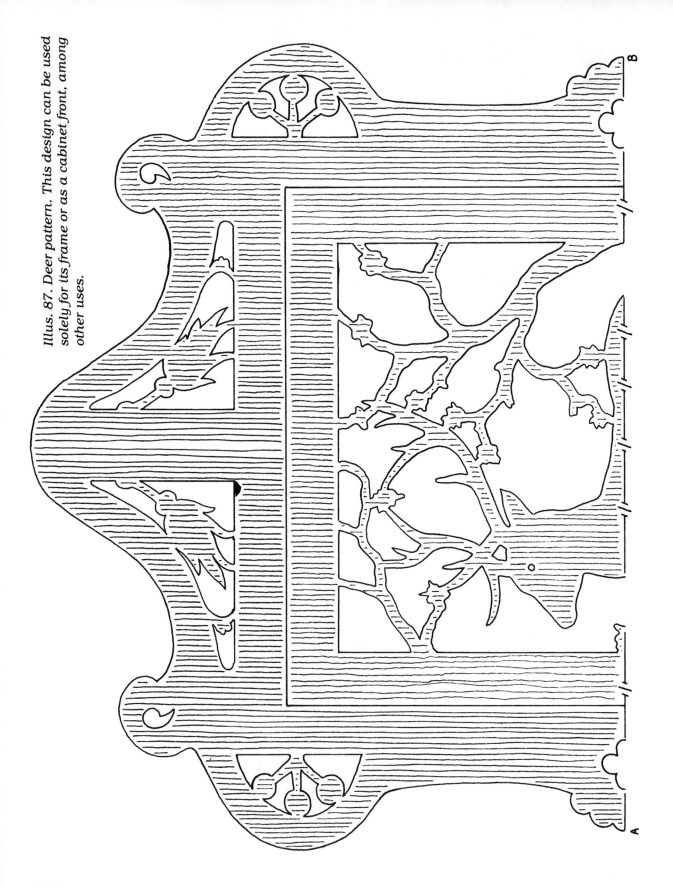

Illus. 87. Deer pattern. This design can be used solely for its frame or as a cabinet front, among other uses.

100

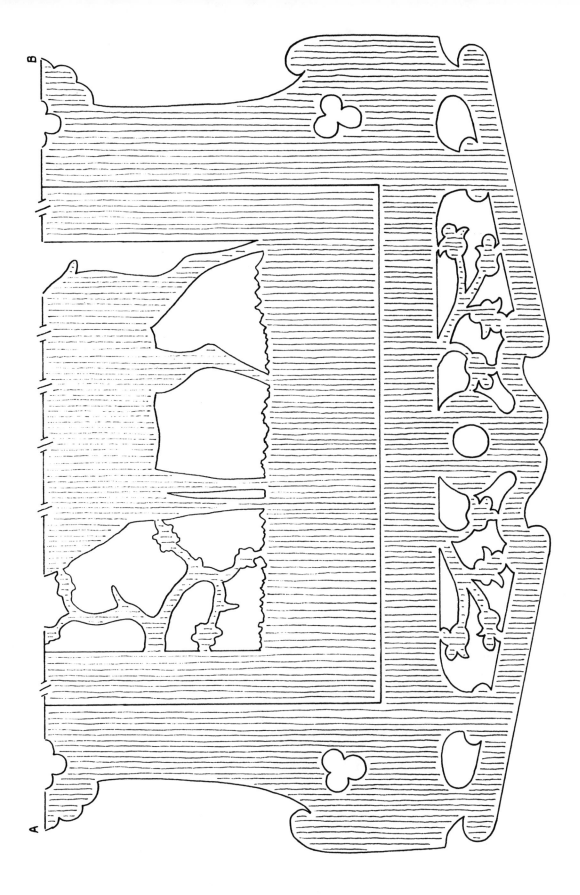

101

Alphabets & Numbers

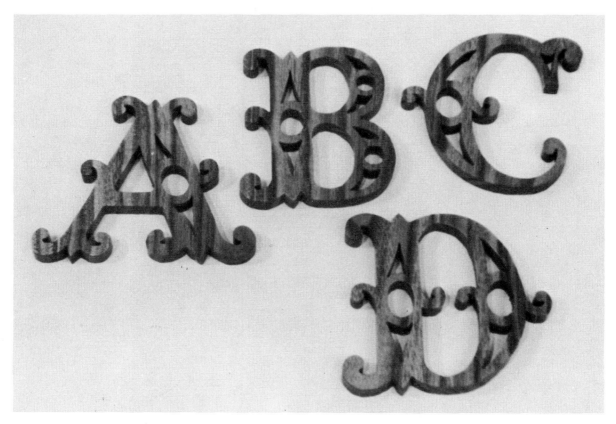

Illus. 88. These are Gay Nineties letters.

Illus. 89. Here, one is applied as an overlay design on a box.

Illus. 90. Pattern for Gay Nineties uppercase letters and numbers. (Continued on the following five pages.)

104

108

Illus. 91. Pattern for Gay Nineties lowercase letters. (Continued on the following two pages.)

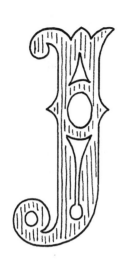

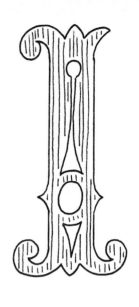

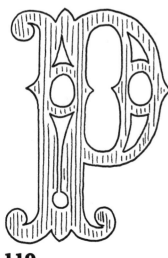
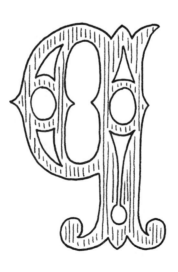

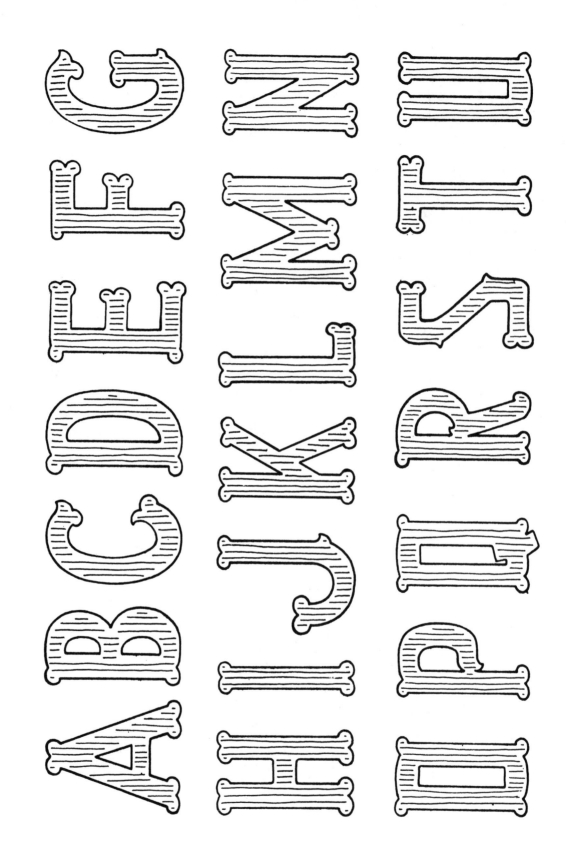

Illus. 92. Pattern for letters and numbers.

112

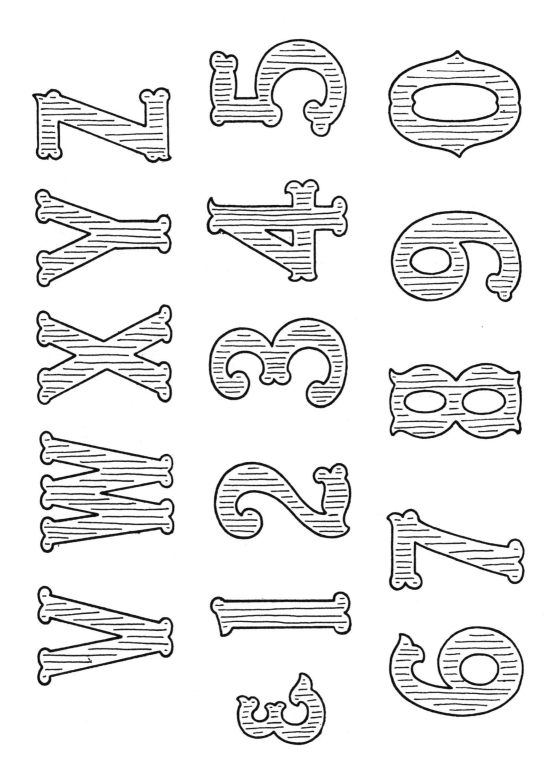

Illus. 93. Simple signs, by Kirk Ratajesak.

Illus. 94. Signboard with Gay Nineties lettering. The top design is optional. (Turn to pages 116–117 for the patterns.)

Illus. 95. Patterns, courtesy of Kirk Ratajesak.

Illus. 96. Signboard pattern. This pattern is designed for one line of letters.

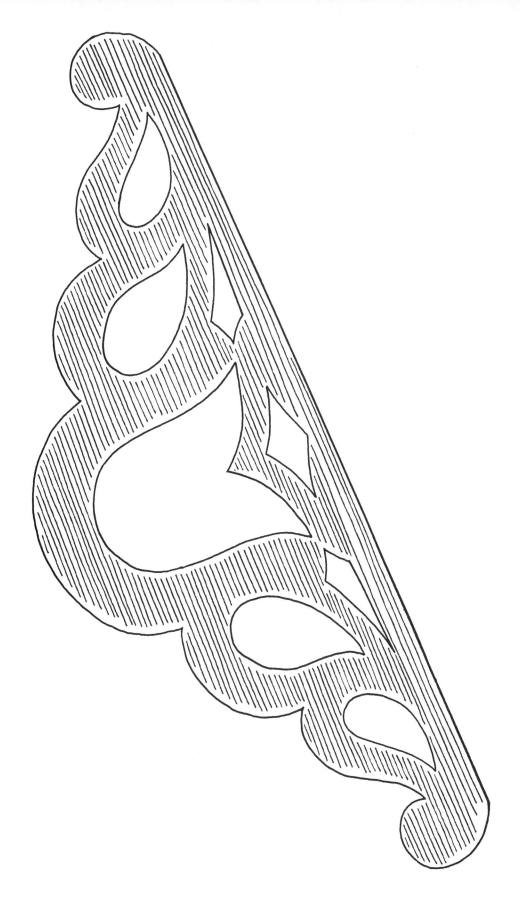

Illus. 97. Pattern for optional signboard ornament.

117

Illus. 98. Signboard pattern, designed for one line of letters.

Illus. 99. Signboard pattern, designed for two lines of letters.

Illus. 100. Single-heart design, by John
Polhemus.

Illus. 101. Single-heart pattern.

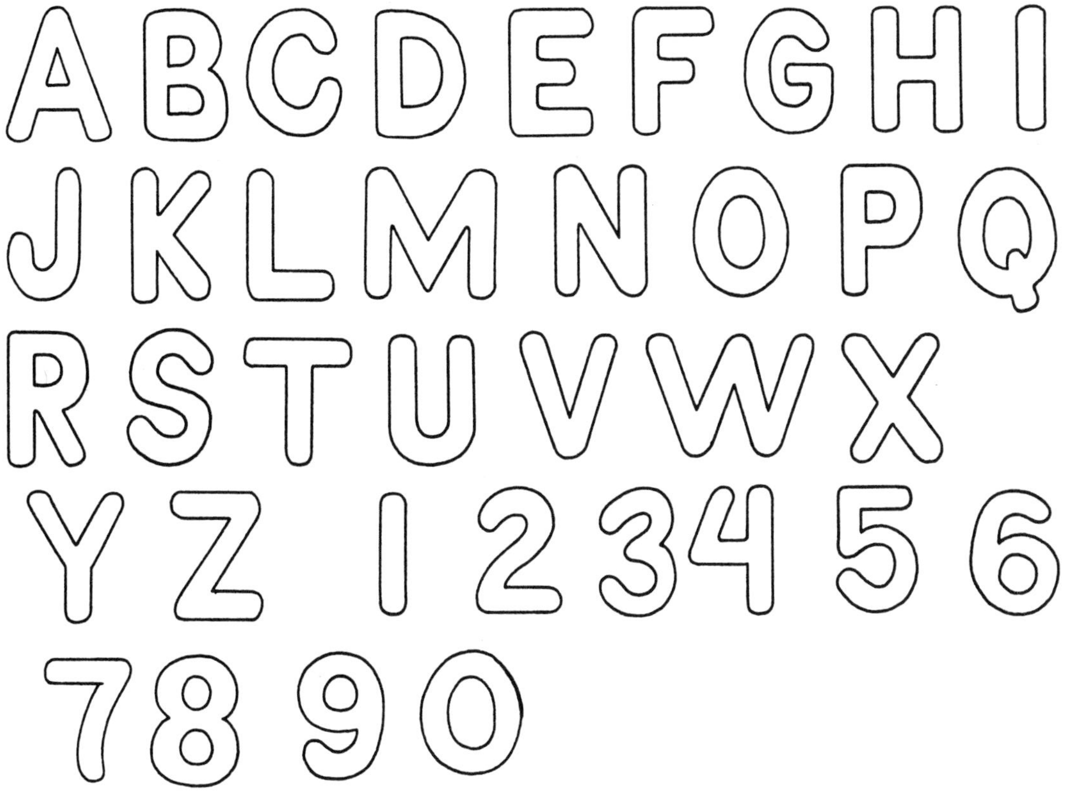
ABCDEFGHI
JKLMNOPQ
RSTUVWX
YZ 123456
7890

Illus. 102. Basic-alphabet pattern.

JOHN POLHEMUS
JOHN POLHEMUS

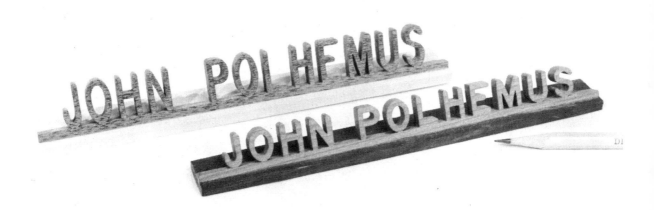

Illus. 103. Desk names, using the same basic alphabet shown in Illus. 102.

Illus. 104. Single heart and arrow, designed by John Polhemus.

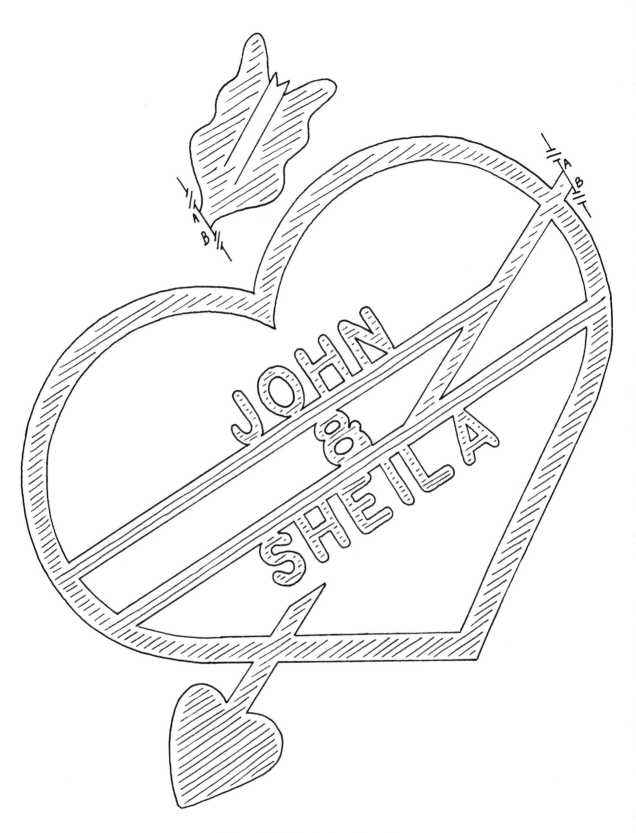

Illus. 105. Single heart and arrow.

Illus. 106. Small desk sign.

Illus. 107. Pattern for small desk sign.

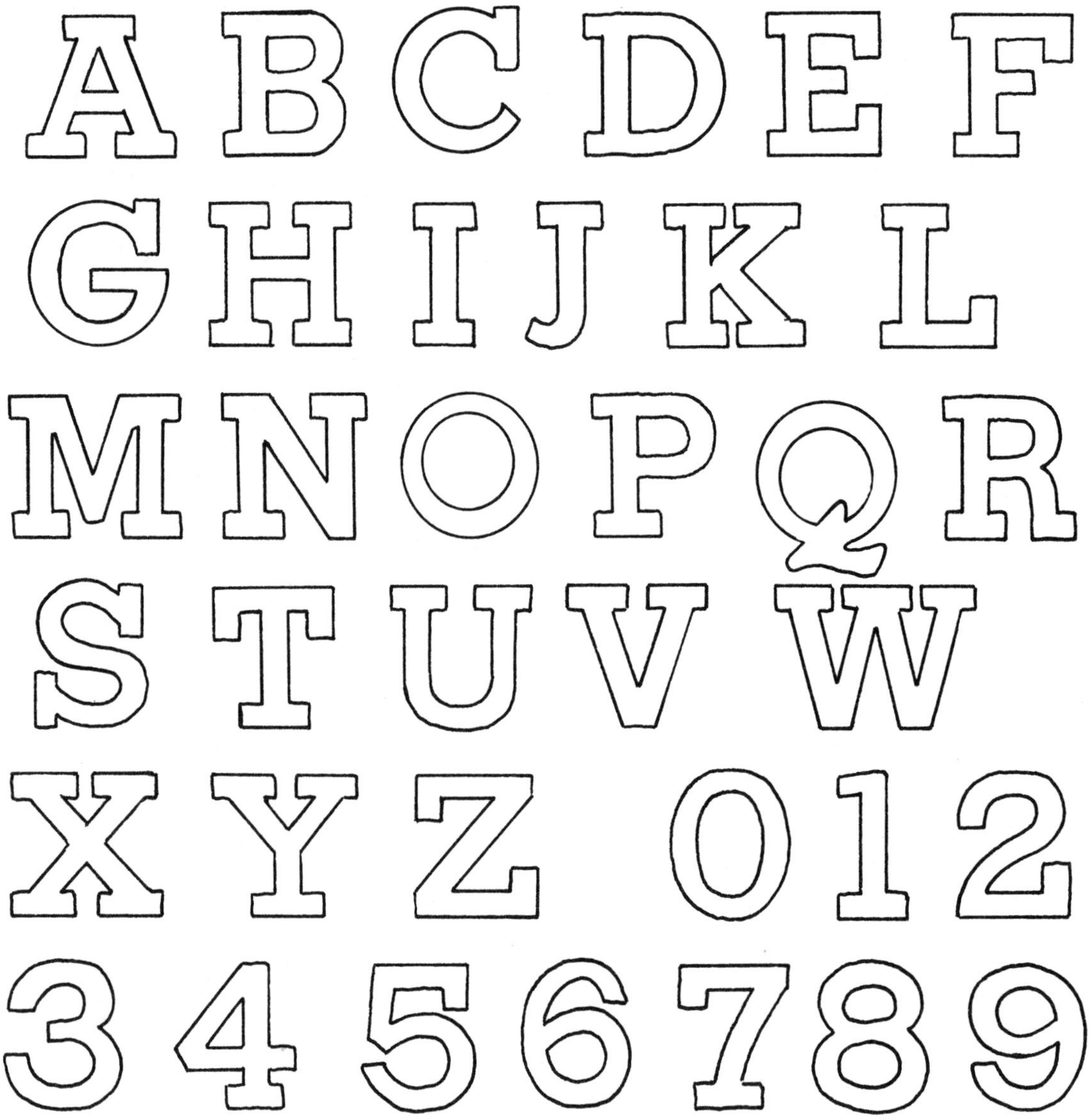

ABCDEF
GHIJKL
MNOPQR
STUVW
XYZ 012
3456789

Illus. 108. Alphabet pattern.

Illus. 109. Double heart and arrow, courtesy of John Polhemus. (The pattern follows.)

Illus. 110. Wedding bells, designed by John Polhemus. (See pages 130–131 for the pattern.)

Illus. 111. Pattern for double heart and arrow.

A

B

KAREN
11 1981

129

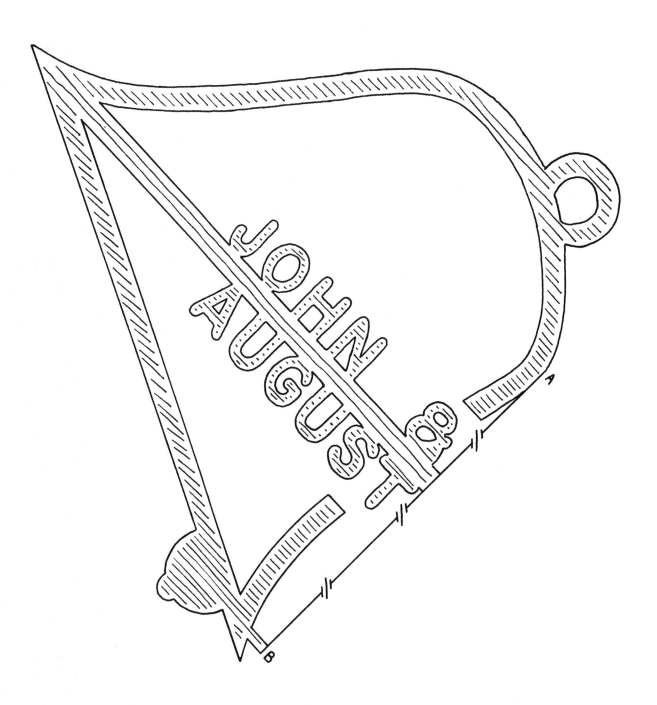

Illus. 112. Wedding bells pattern.

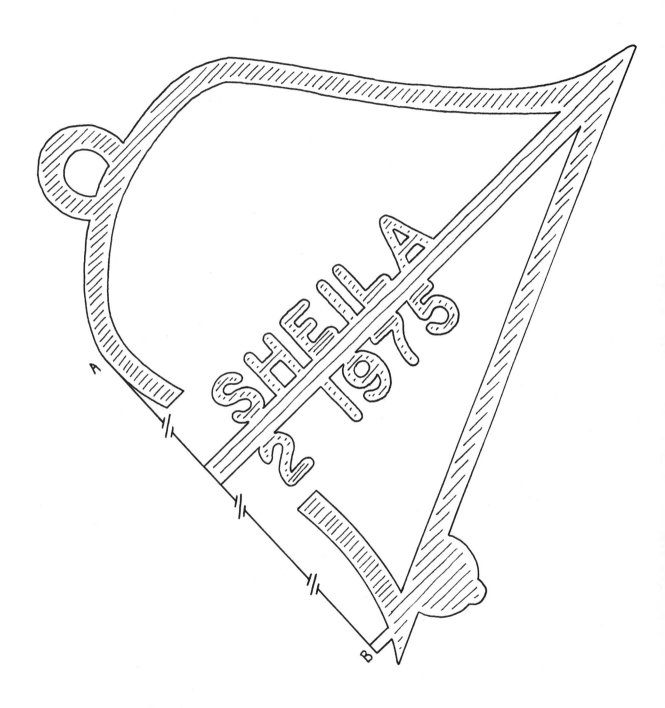

Illus. 113. Pattern for sign with posts. The posts can be turned and slotted or halved. Or, the entire pattern can simply be sawn out of flat stock.

132

Illus. 114. Family tree, developed by John Polhemus. (The pattern follows.)

134

Illus. 115. Family-tree pattern.

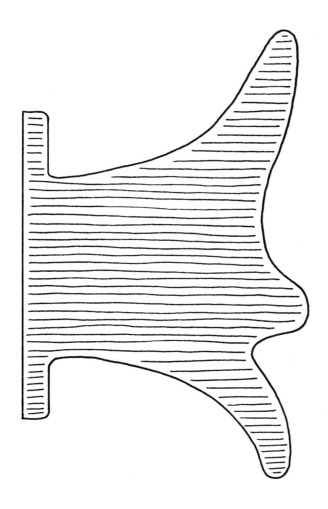

Illus. 116. Pattern for sign with bird and flowers. The shaded areas indicate glued-on overlays.

Shelves

Illus. 117. This photo shows how one basic bracket design (lower middle) can be used to make several different kinds of shelves. When making corner shelves, add the thickness of the stock along one edge of just one bracket member to allow for the overlap of a simple nailed butt joint. Corner shelves are one fourth of a circle. Wall shelves can be made to whatever length you desire between brackets.

Illus. 118. Bracket pattern for shelves shown in Illus. 117.

139

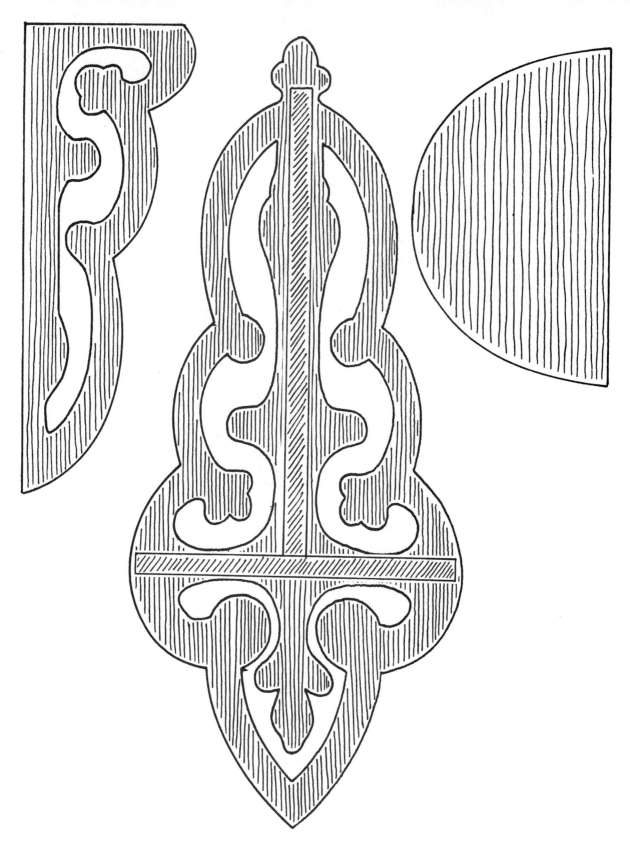

Illus. 119. Shelf pattern.

Illus. 120. Shelf design, by Kirk Ratajesak. (The pattern follows.)

141

A   B

Illus. 121. Shelf pattern. (Continued on the next page.)

142

A   B

Illus. 122. Shelf pattern.

Illus. 123. Shelf design. (See pages 146–147 for the pattern.)

Illus. 124. Shelf design, by Kirk Ratajesak. (See pages 148–149 for the pattern.)

Illus. 125. Shelf pattern.

Illus. 126. Shelf pattern.

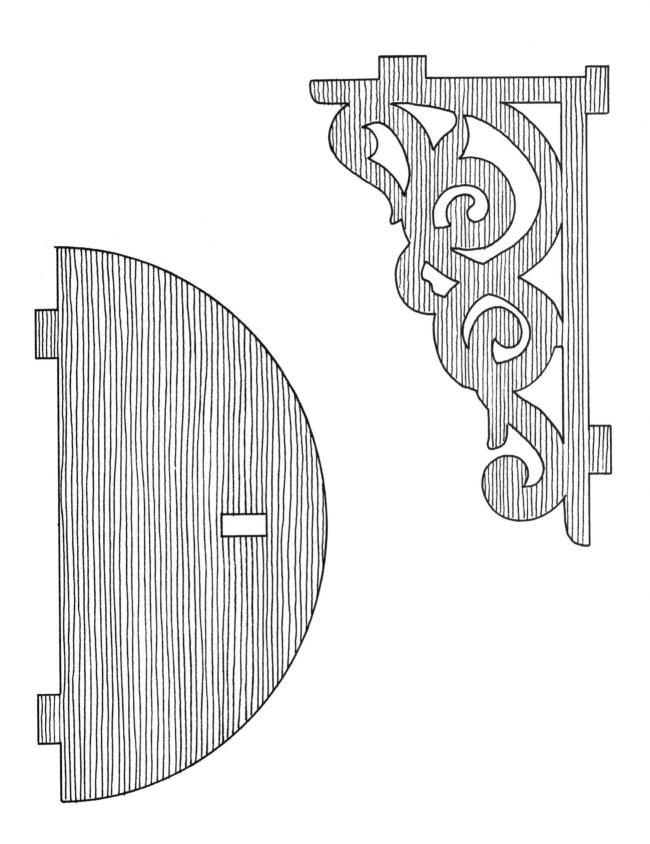

Illus. 127. Shelf design, by Kirk Ratajesak.

Illus. 128. Shelf pattern. (Continued on the next page.)

A   B

151

Illus. 129. Shelf pattern.
(Continued on the next page.)

A

B

A.

B.

153

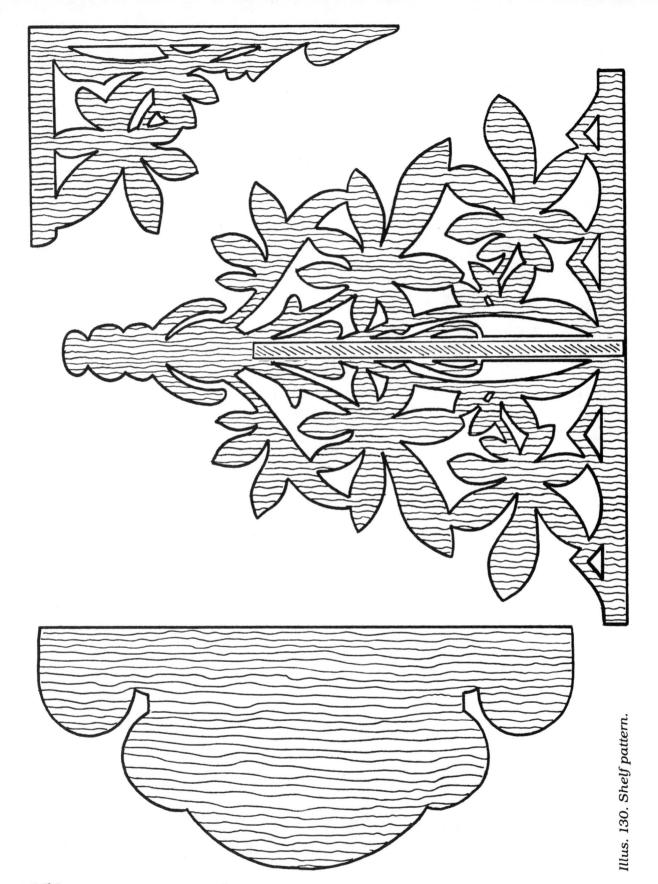

Illus. 130. Shelf pattern.

154

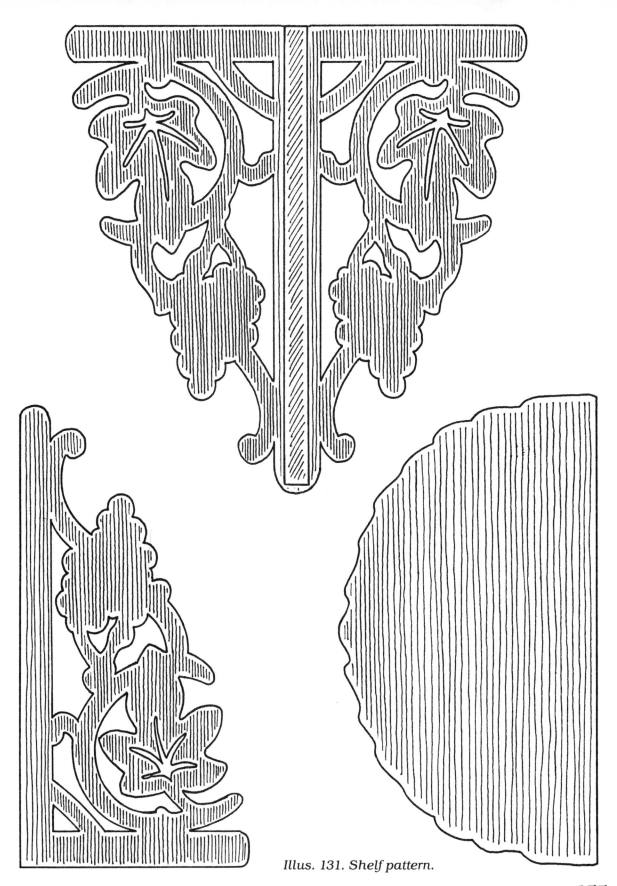

Illus. 131. Shelf pattern.

155

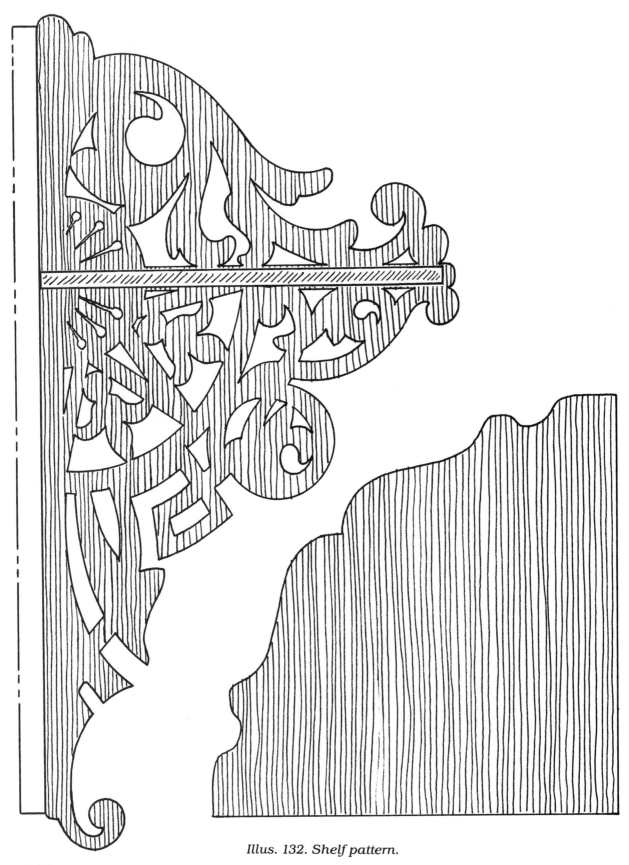

Illus. 132. Shelf pattern.

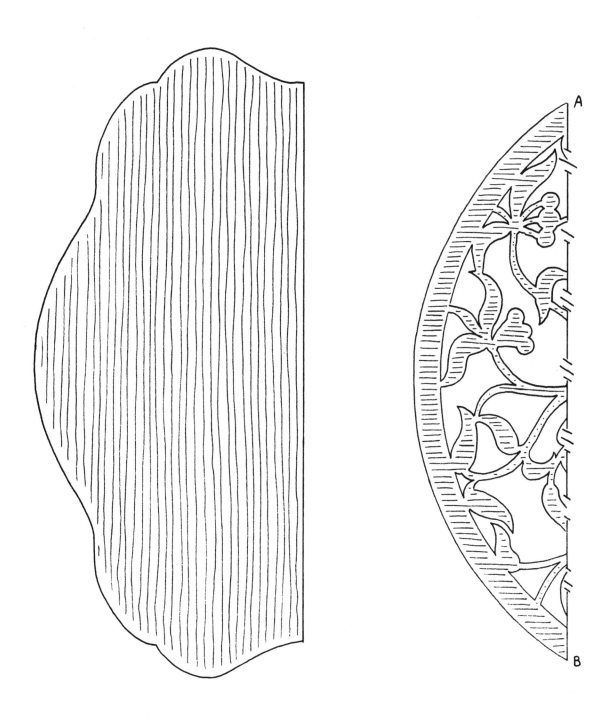

Illus. 133. Shelf pattern. (Continued on the next two pages.)

158

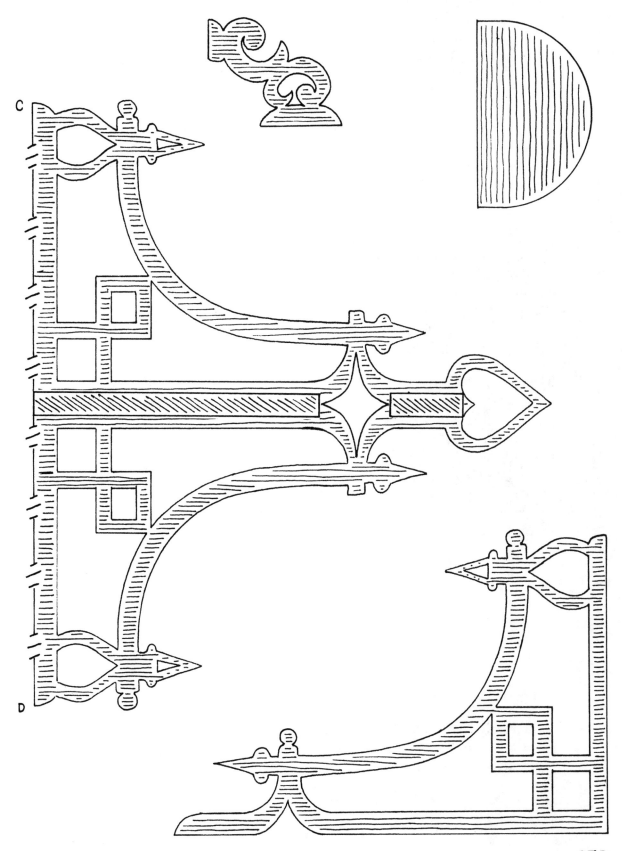

159

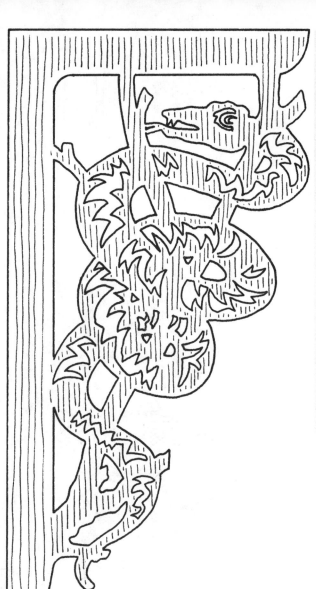

Illus. 134. Snake shelf, made by Carl Weckhorst.

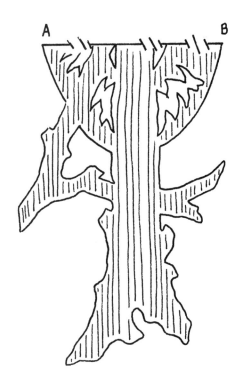

Illus. 135. Snake-shelf pattern. (Continued on the next page.)

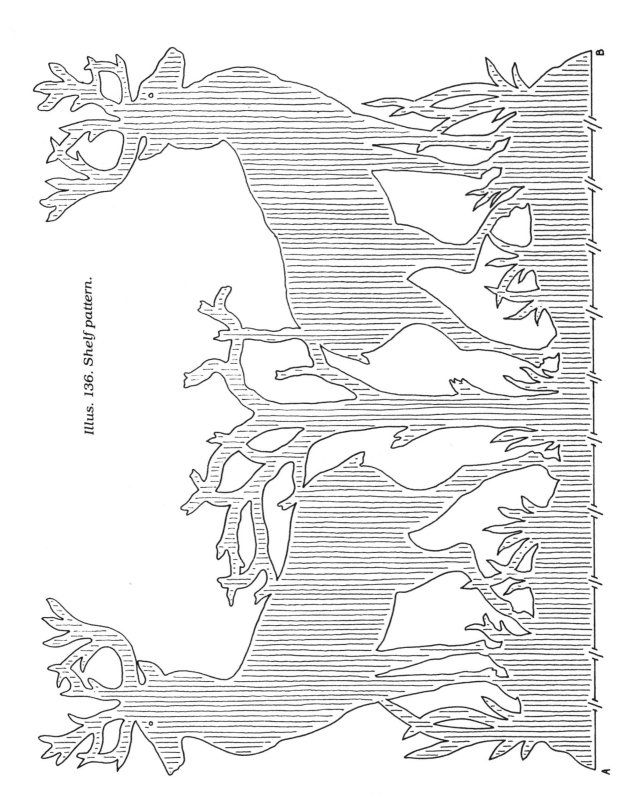

Illus. 136. Shelf pattern.

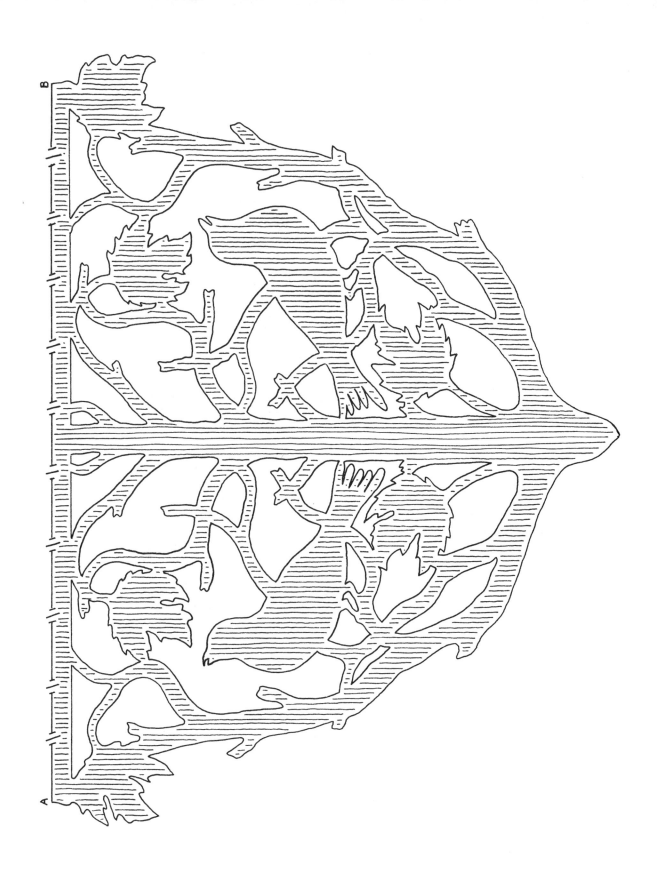

163

Illus. 137. Shelf pattern.
(Continued on the next two pages.)

164

B

A

Illus. 138. Shelf pattern.
(Continued on the next three pages.)

B

A

167

168

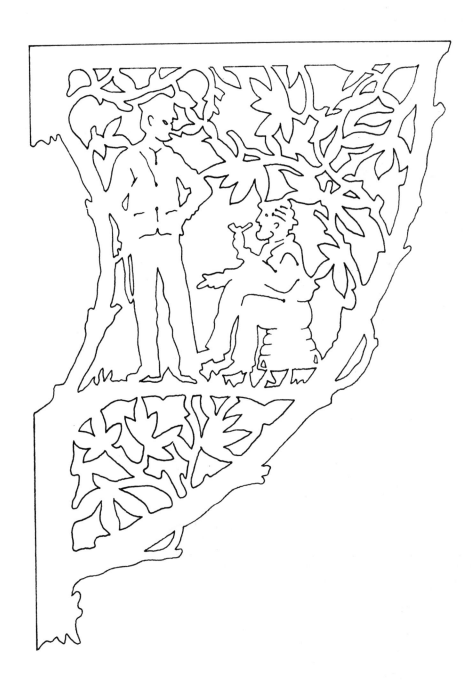

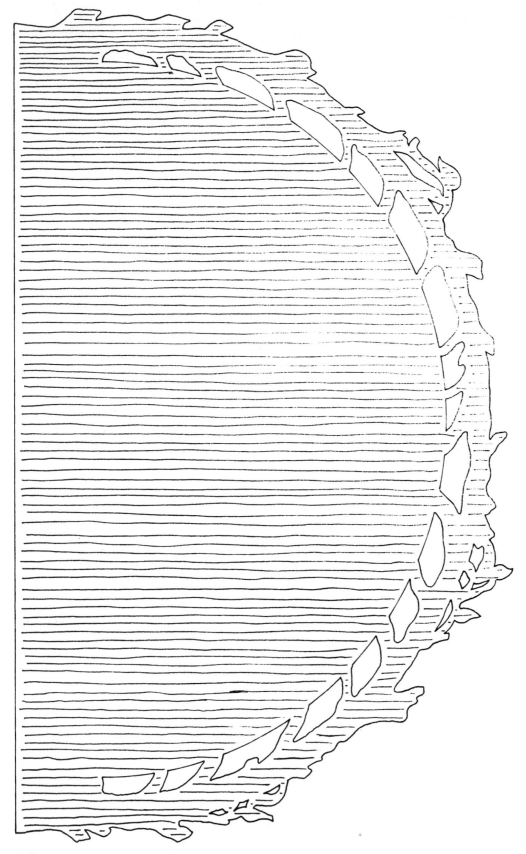

170

Illus. 139. Shelf pattern.

Delicate Brackets

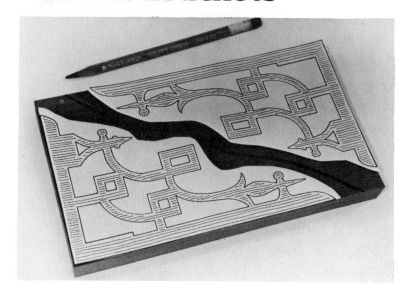

Illus. 140. Preparing brackets for sawing. Note that the straight edges are cut square to each other and the pattern is applied to these presawn straight edges. Also, note how brackets can be laid out to conserve stock.

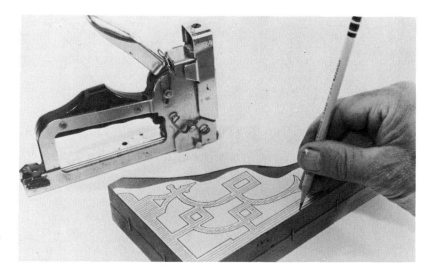

Illus. 141. Here, the stock is rough-sawn, aligned, stacked, and stapled along the edges for sawing one pair of identical brackets at once.

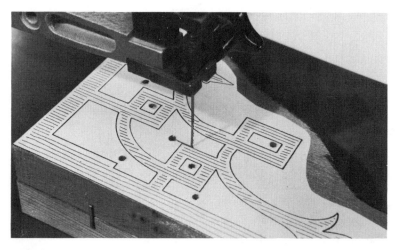

Illus. 142. Starting the inside cuts. Note the hole locations so that the cut can quickly proceed into a starting corner.

Illus. 143. Bracket patterns.

Illus. 144. Bracket patterns.

Illus. 145. Bracket patterns.

Illus. 146. Bracket patterns.

Illus. 147. Bracket patterns.

Illus. 148. Bracket patterns.

Architectural Brackets

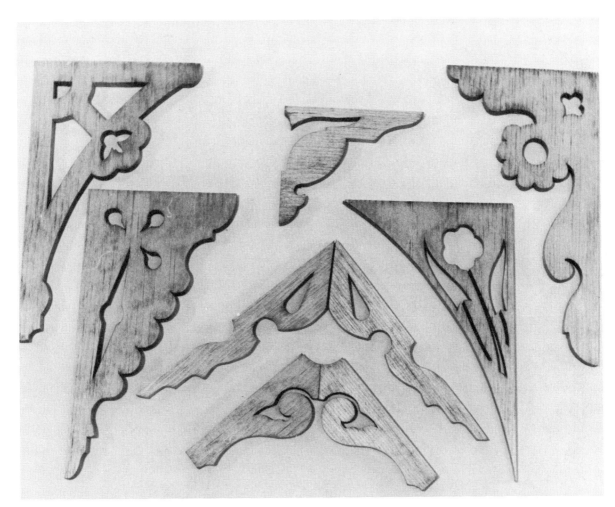

Illus. 149. These brackets are usually cut from thicker material—say, ½" to 1", or thicker.

Illus. 150. Bracket patterns.

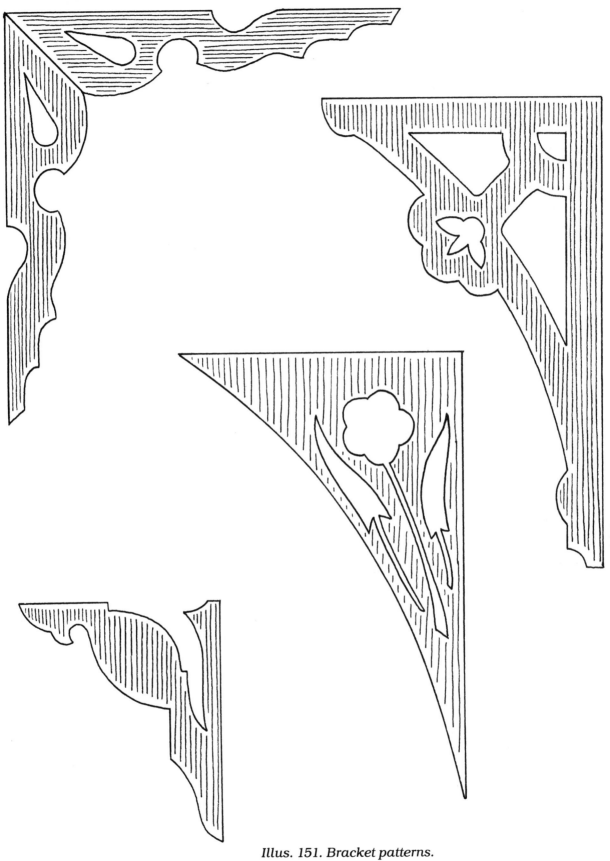

Illus. 151. Bracket patterns.

181

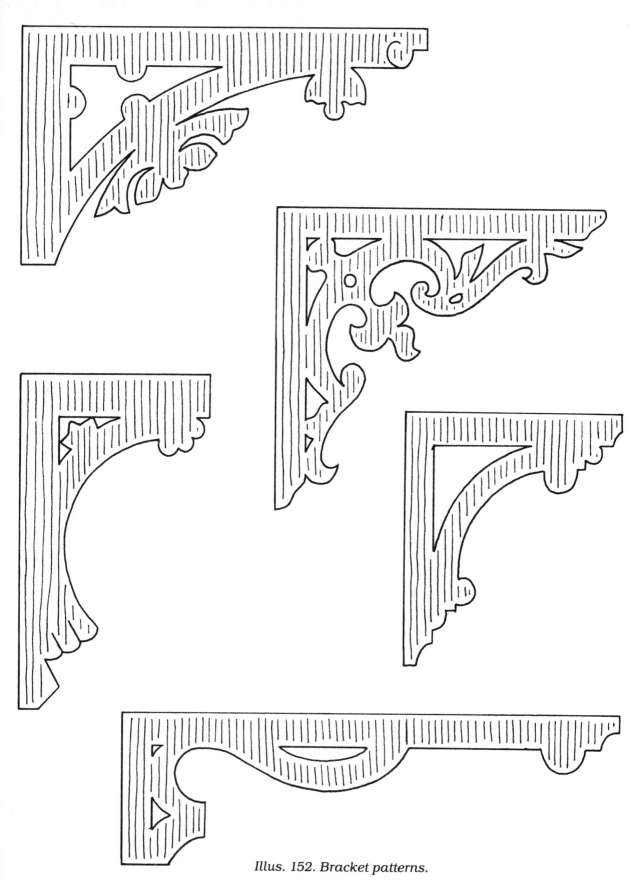

Illus. 152. Bracket patterns.

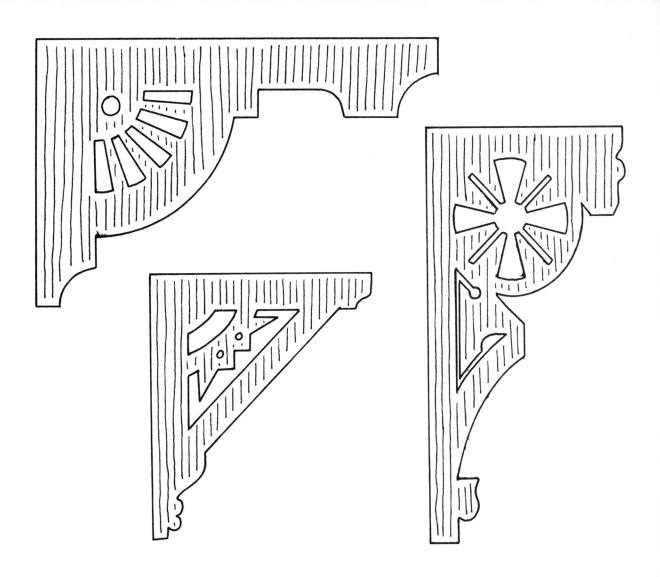

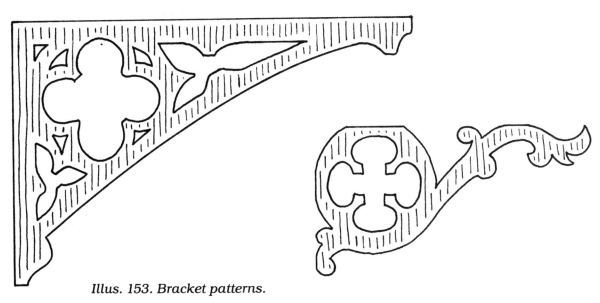

Illus. 153. Bracket patterns.

Balusters

Illus. 154. Baluster patterns.

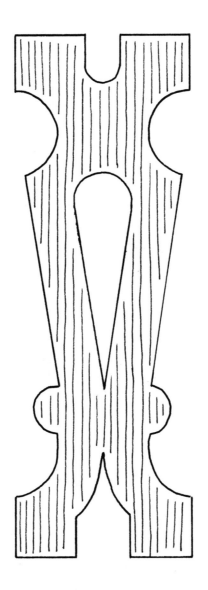

Running Trim

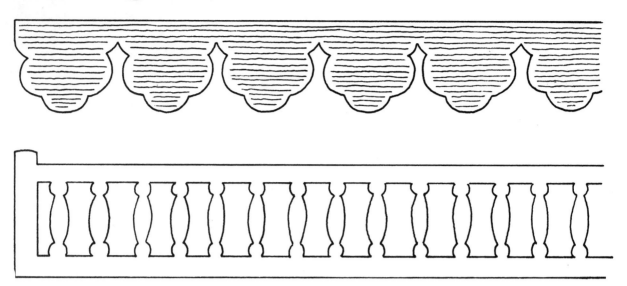

Illus. 155. Trim patterns.

Illus. 156. Trim patterns.

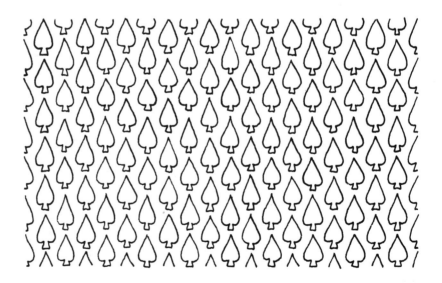

Illus. 157. Trim patterns.

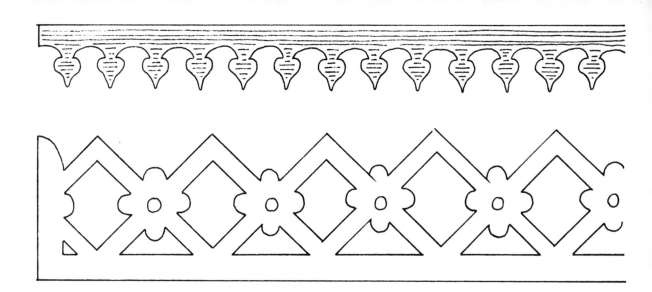

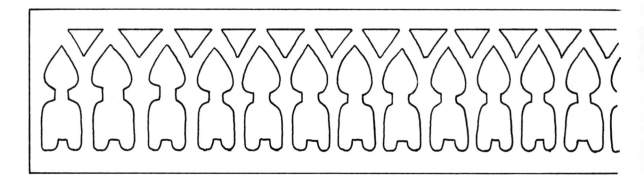

Illus. 158. Trim patterns.

Victorian Arches

Illus. 159. Victorian arch.

Illus. 160. Victorian arch application.

Illus. 161. Victorian arch pattern. (Continued on the next page.)

A

B

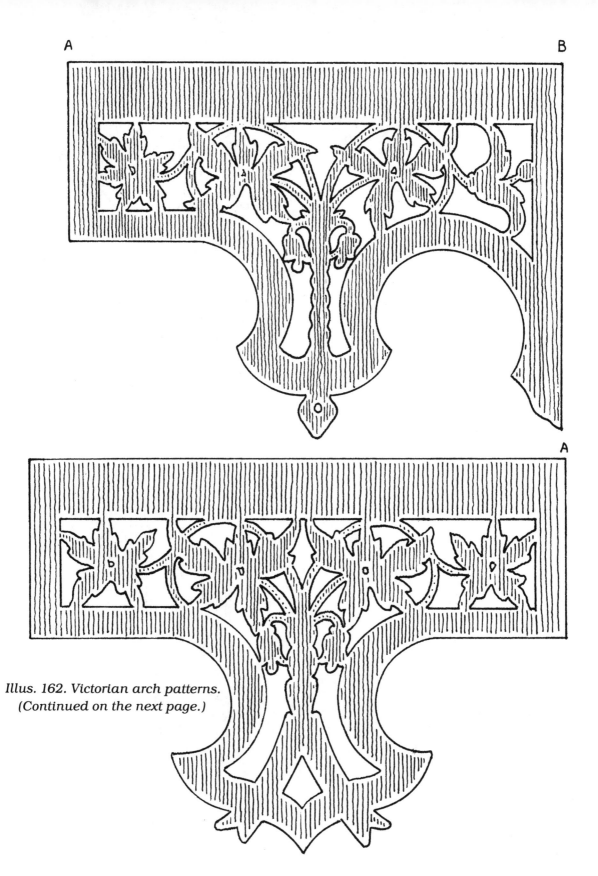

Illus. 162. Victorian arch patterns.
(Continued on the next page.)

193

Gable Ornaments

Illus. 163. Gable-ornament pattern.

Illus. 164. Gable-ornament pattern.

Illus. 165. Gable-ornament pattern.

197

Grilles

Illus. 166. Grille pattern.

Illus. 167. Grille pattern.

Illus. 168. Grille patterns.

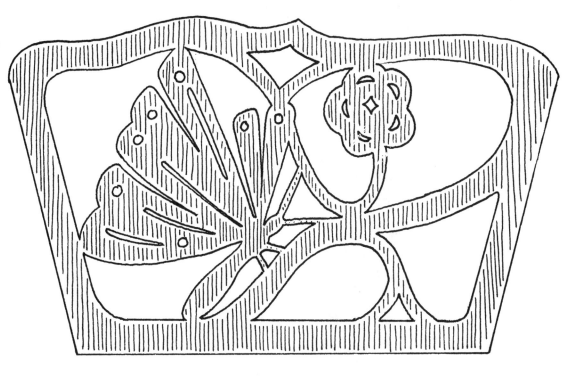

Illus. 169. Grille patterns.

Inlays & Overlays

Illus. 171. Heart-shaped pattern for inlay or overlay.

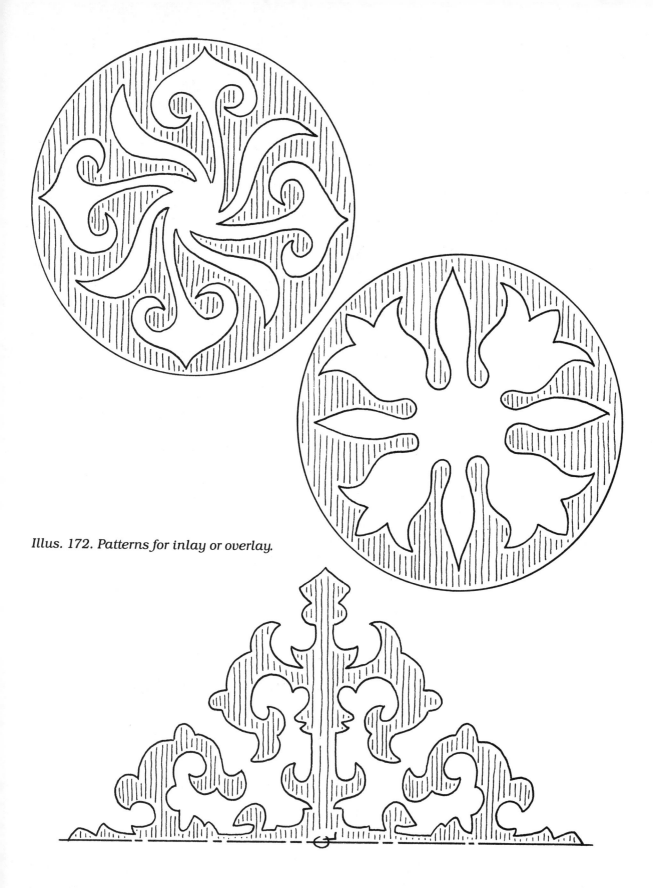

Illus. 172. Patterns for inlay or overlay.

Illus. 173. Heart-shaped pattern for inlay or overlay.

Illus. 174. Oval floral pattern for inlay or overlay.

206

Illus. 175. Floral pattern for inlay or overlay.

Illus. 176. Pattern for inlay or overlay.

Christmas Ornaments

Illus. 177. Christmas ornament patterns.

Illus. 178. Pattern for reindeer and sleigh.

Arrows

Illus. 179. Arrow patterns.

Nautical Silhouettes

Illus. 180. Nautical silhouette pattern.

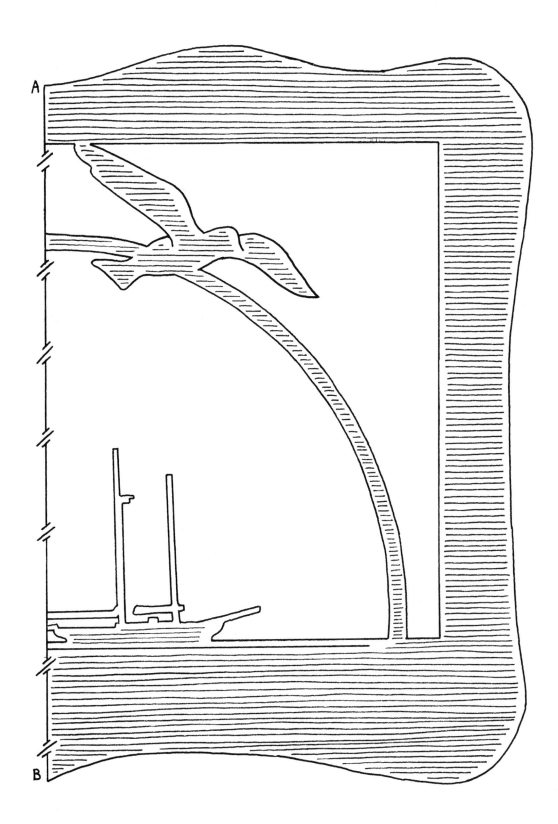

A

B

213

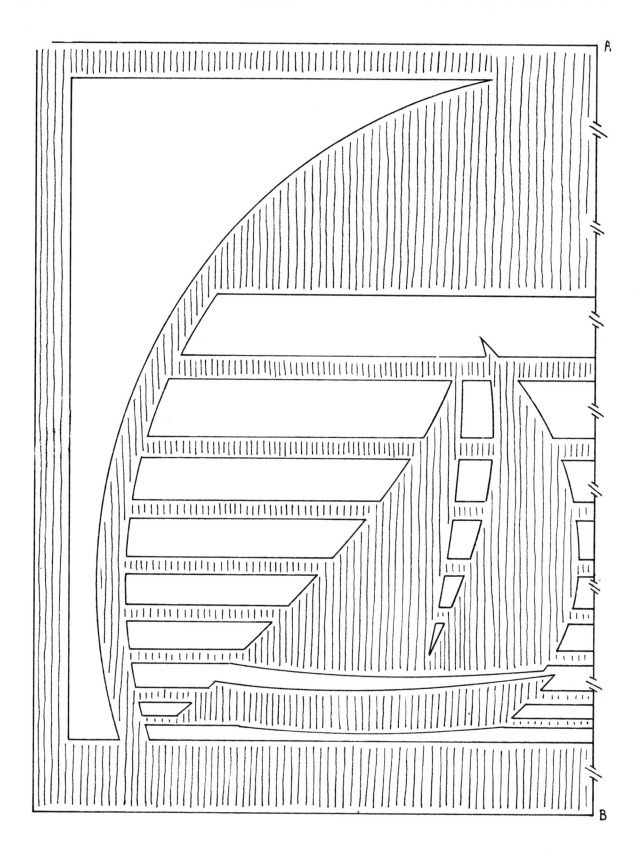

Illus. 181. Nautical silhouette pattern.

214

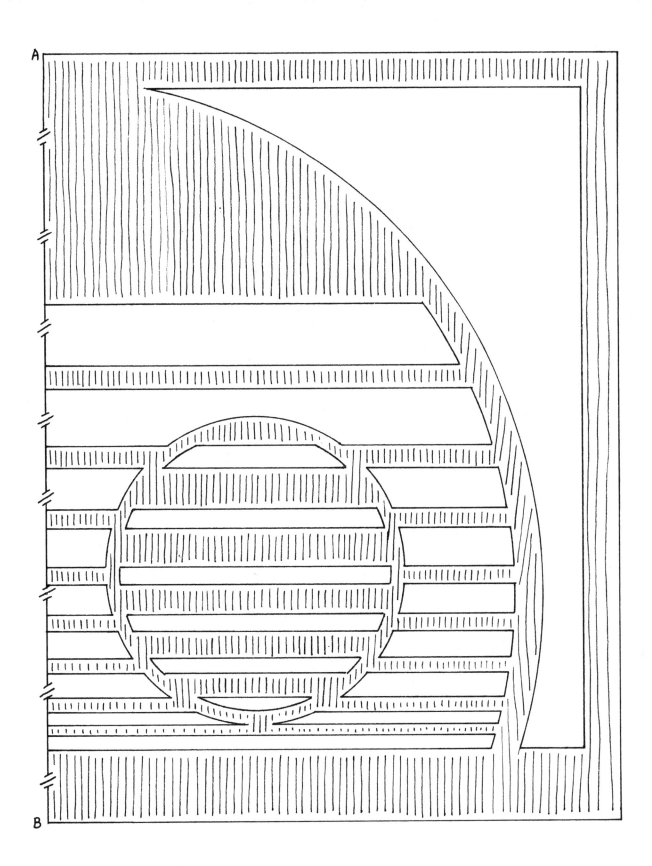

215

Wheels

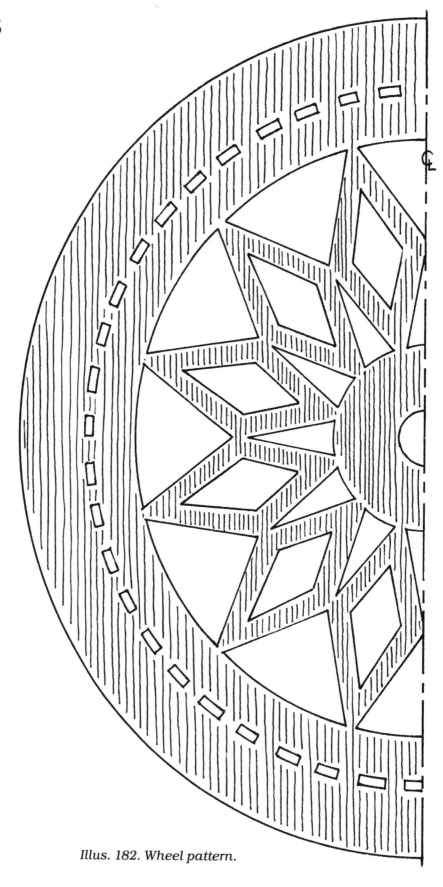

Illus. 182. Wheel pattern.

Illus. 183. Wheel patterns.

Vehicles

Illus. 184. Old-fashioned touring car, courtesy of AMI Limited.

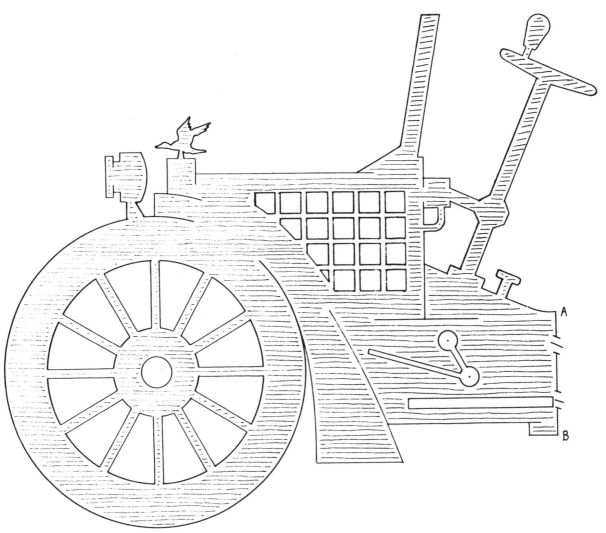

Illus. 185. Touring-car pattern. Adapted from AMI Pattern Book #1,
copyright Advanced Machinery Imports Ltd.

A

B

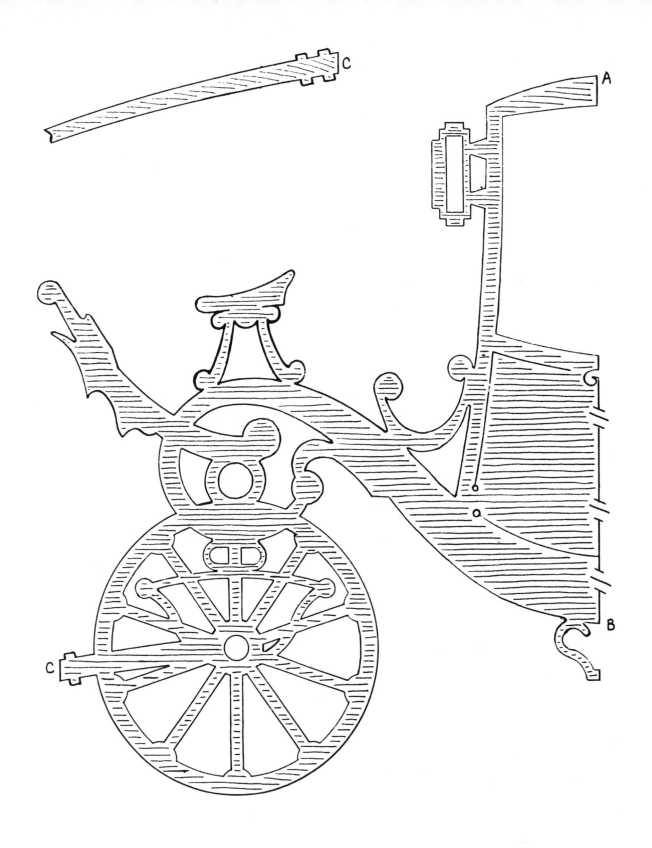

Illus. 186. Carriage pattern. Adapted from AMI Pattern Book #1, *copyright Advanced Machinery Imports Ltd.*

A

B

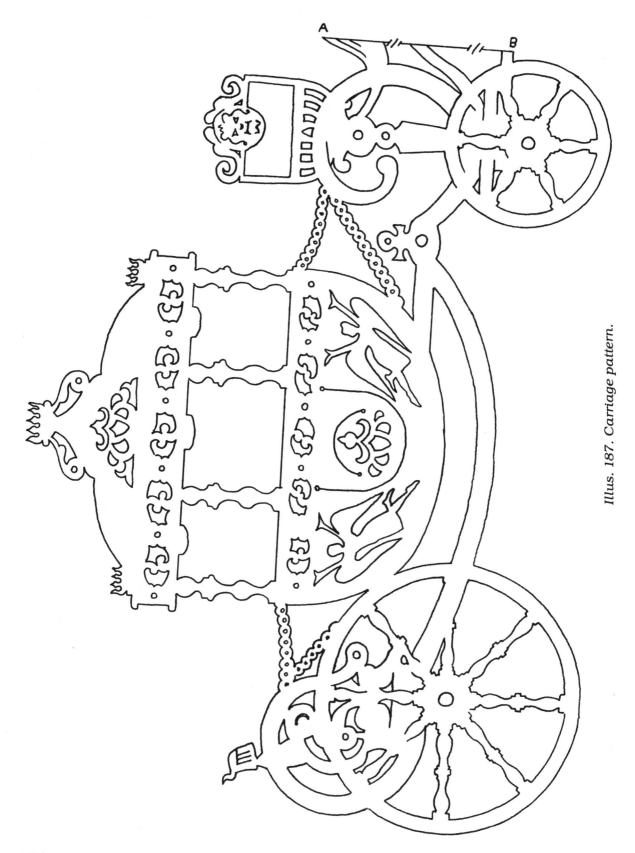

Illus. 187. Carriage pattern.

A

B

223

Miniatures

224

226

Clocks

Illus. 189. This is a simple one-piece scroll-sawn clock-face cut from plywood. (The pattern is on the next page.)

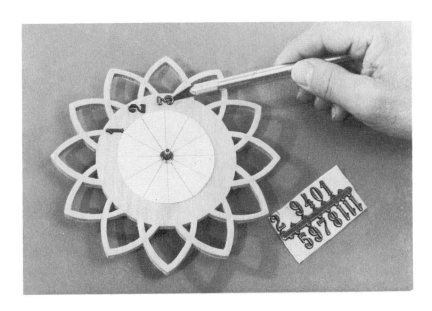

Illus. 190. Stick-on numbers are another option.

Illus. 191. Clock pattern.

Illus. 192. Clock pattern.

229

Illus. 193. Clock face pattern. Battery-operated movements (see Illus. 196), hands, dials, and so on, are available from many mail-order sources, including the Klockit Co., Inc., Box 629, Lake Geneva, WI 53147, and Reidle Products, Box 58, Yuba, WI 54634.

230

Illus. 194. Wall clock, de-signed by Kirk Ratajesak. (Turn to pages 234—237 for the pattern.)

*Illus. 195. Assemble the
pieces with glue and brads.*

Illus. 196. A simple battery-operated movement is inexpensive and easy to install.

Illus. 197. Placing the time ring on the wall clock. This clock requires a 3¾"-diameter styrene time ring, available from the Klockit Co., Inc. and from Reidle Products.

Illus. 198. Colored material, such as poster paper, placed behind a cutout area provides contrast to the wood. This idea can be applied to many other fretwork projects.

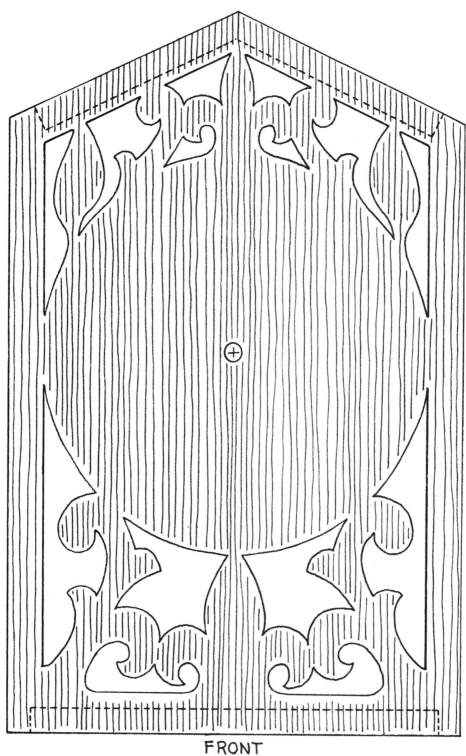

FRONT

Illus. 199. Wall-clock pattern. (Continued on the next three pages.)

ROOF
FILLER
(2 Pieces)

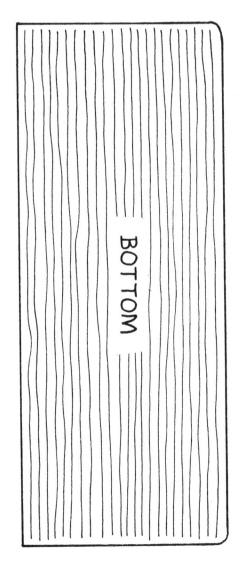

BOTTOM

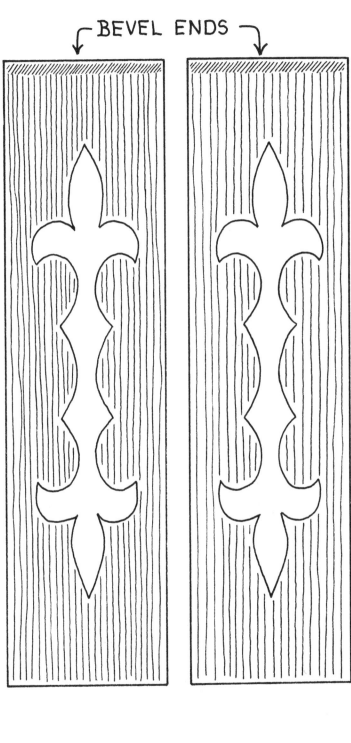

BEVEL ENDS

A

B

BOTTOM FILLER

236

ROOF
(2 Pieces)

BOTTOM FILLER

BOTTOM

BACK

A

B

Illus. 200. German-style wall clock. This clock requires a 4⅜"-diameter cuckoo-clock dial, available from Kienzle Time, Inc., P.O. Box 98, 100 Honing Rd., Fox Lake, IL 60020, or from Reidle Products. *(Turn to pages 240–243 for the pattern.)*

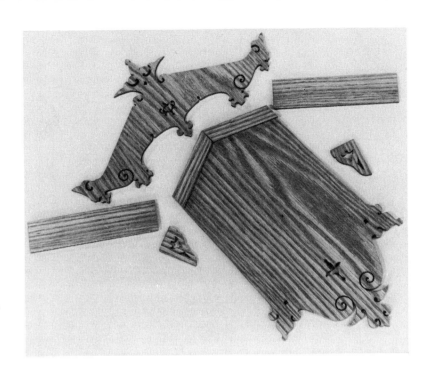

Illus. 201. All the pieces of the German-style wall clock. The starting assembly has the two upper filler boards glued in place.

Illus. 202. Next, you attach the decorative scroll top onto the filler boards.

239

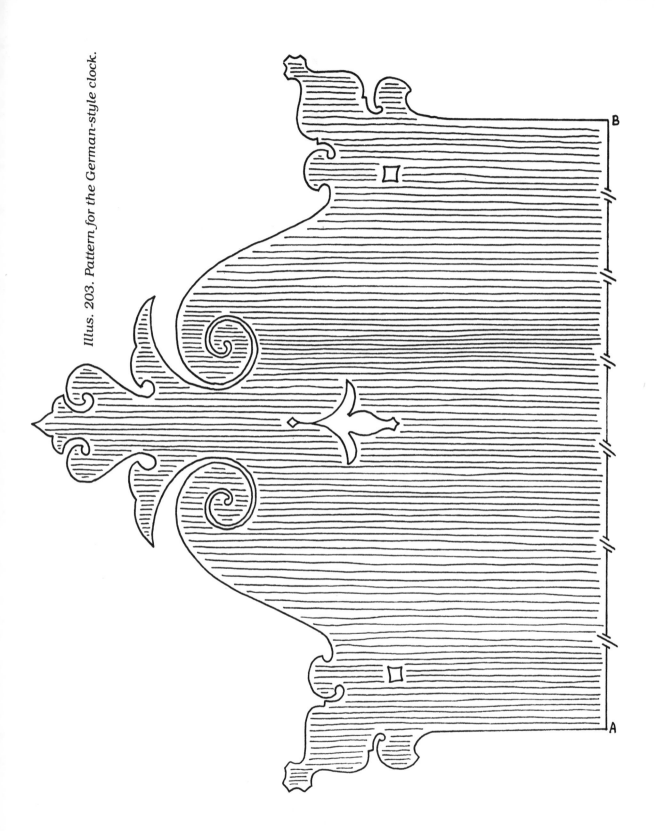

Illus. 203. Pattern for the German-style clock.

B

A

240

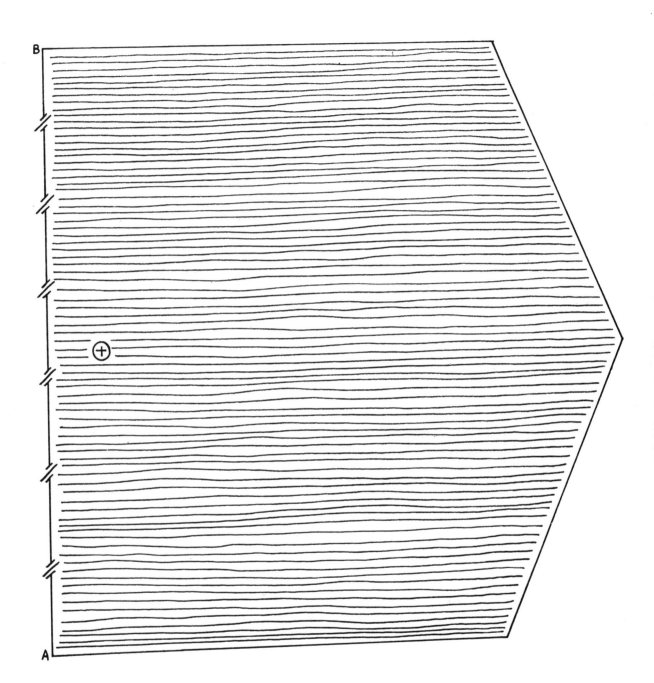

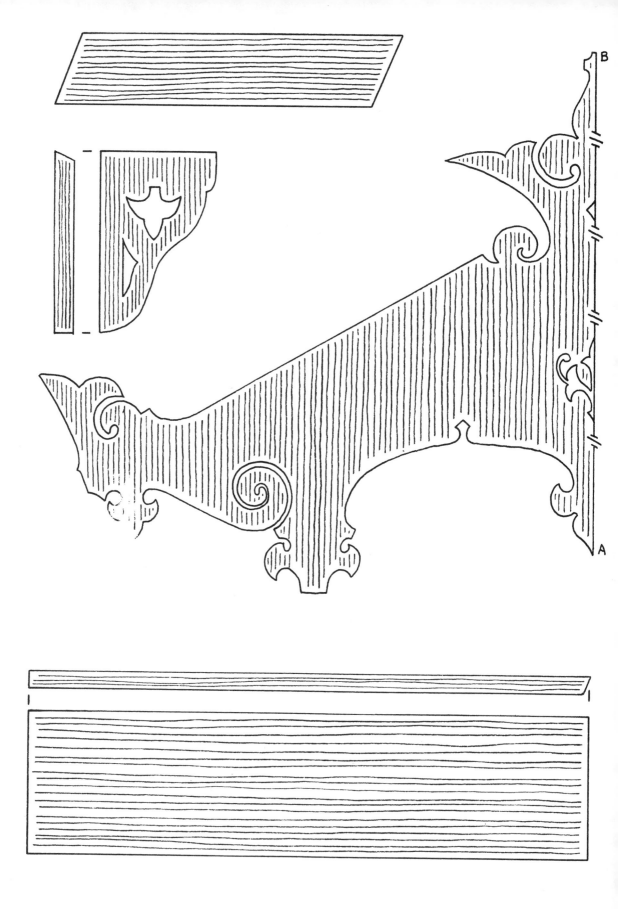

242

B

A

243

Illus. 204. Exploded view of the clock assembly.

Miscellaneous Patterns

Illus. 205. Circular rose pattern.

Illus. 206. This repeating
pattern makes an interesting
chessboard or checkerboard.
The board is made up of two
layers. The top layer is fret-
cut and glued onto a con-
trasting plain panel.

Illus. 207. Four identical patterns comprise the chess- or
checkerboard layout.

Illus. 208. Cutting out the
board.

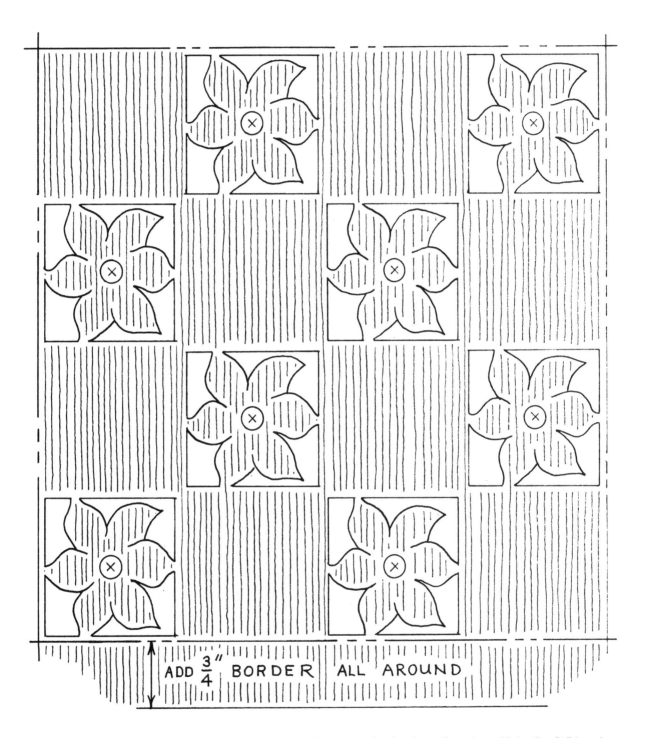

ADD ¾″ BORDER ALL AROUND

Illus. 209. One fourth of the pattern for the chess- or checkerboard project. Note the ¾″ border all around. A 13¾″ square of material is required.

Illus. 210. Mandala-like patterns.

Illus. 211. Grille pattern and pattern for a 16th-century explorer.

249

METRIC EQUIVALENCY CHART

MM—MILLIMETRES   CM—CENTIMETRES

INCHES TO MILLIMETRES AND CENTIMETRES

INCHES	MM	CM	INCHES	CM	INCHES	CM
⅛	3	0.3	9	22.9	30	76.2
¼	6	0.6	10	25.4	31	78.7
⅜	10	1.0	11	27.9	32	81.3
½	13	1.3	12	30.5	33	83.8
⅝	16	1.6	13	33.0	34	86.4
¾	19	1.9	14	35.6	35	88.9
⅞	22	2.2	15	38.1	36	91.4
1	25	2.5	16	40.6	37	94.0
1¼	32	3.2	17	43.2	38	96.5
1½	38	3.8	18	45.7	39	99.1
1¾	44	4.4	19	48.3	40	101.6
2	51	5.1	20	50.8	41	104.1
2½	64	6.4	21	53.3	42	106.7
3	76	7.6	22	55.9	43	109.2
3½	89	8.9	23	58.4	44	111.8
4	102	10.2	24	61.0	45	114.3
4½	114	11.4	25	63.5	46	116.8
5	127	12.7	26	66.0	47	119.4
6	152	15.2	27	68.6	48	121.9
7	178	17.8	28	71.1	49	124.5
8	203	20.3	29	73.7	50	127.0

About the Authors

Patrick Spielman's love of wood began when, as a child, he transformed fruit crates into toys. Now this prolific and innovative woodworker is respected worldwide as a teacher and author.

His most famous contribution to the woodworking field has been his perfection of a method to season green wood with polyethylene glycol 1000 (PEG). He went on to invent, manufacture, and distribute the PEG-Thermovat chemical seasoning system.

During his many years as shop instructor in Wisconsin, Spielman published manuals, teaching guides, and more than 14 popular books, including *Modern Wood Technology*, a college text. He also wrote six educational series on wood technology, tool use, processing techniques, design, and wood-product planning.

Author of the best-selling *Router Handbook* (over 600,000 copies sold), Spielman has served as editorial consultant to a professional magazine, and his products, techniques, and many books have been featured in numerous periodicals.

This pioneer of new ideas and inventor of countless jigs, fixtures, and designs used throughout the world is a unique combination of expert woodworker and brilliant teacher—all of which have endeared him to his many readers and to his publisher.

At Spielmans Wood Works in the woods of northern Door County, Wisconsin, he and his family create and sell some of the most durable and popular furniture products and designs available.

Coauthor James Reidle has been doing fancy woodwork along with general carpentry work all his life. He grew up watching his father create magnificent pieces of scroll-saw fretwork on treadle-type scroll saws. Years later, he wanted to recapture the best features of the early scroll saws his father used, so he developed one of his own, which is especially designed for fretwork and fine-detail scroll sawing. In addition, Reidle developed the first mail-order business in a number of years that is mainly devoted to fretwork patterns and supplies.

Should you wish to contact Patrick Spielman or James Reidle, please send your letters to Sterling Publishing Company.

CHARLES NURNBERG
STERLING PUBLISHING COMPANY

251

Current Books by Patrick Spielman

Alphabets and Designs for Wood Signs. 50 alphabet patterns, plans for many decorative designs, the latest on hand carving, routing, cutouts, and sandblasting. Pricing data. Photo gallery (4 pages in color) of wood signs by professionals from across the U.S. Over 200 illustrations. 128 pages.

Carving Large Birds. Spielman and renowned woodcarver Bill Dehos show how to carve a fascinating array of large birds. All of the tools and basic techniques that are used are discussed in depth, and hundreds of photos, illustrations, and patterns are provided for carving graceful swans, majestic eagles, comical-looking penguins, a variety of owls, and scores of other birds. Oversized. 16 pages in full color. 192 pages.

Carving Wild Animals: Life-Size Wood Figures. Spielman and renowned woodcarver Bill Dehos show how to carve more than 20 magnificent creatures of the North American wild. A cougar, black bear, prairie dog, squirrel, raccoon, and fox are some of the life-size animals included. Step-by-

step, photo-filled instructions and multiple-view patterns, plus tips on the use of tools, wood selection, finishing, and polishing help you bring each animal to life. Oversized. Over 300 photos; 16 pages in full color. 240 pages.

Gluing & Clamping. A thorough, up-to-date examination of one of the most critical steps in woodworking. Spielman explores the features of every type of glue—from traditional animal-hide glues to the newest epoxies—the clamps and tools needed, the bonding properties of different wood species, safety tips, and all techniques from edge-to-edge and end-to-end gluing to applying plastic laminates. Also included is a glossary of terms. Over 500 illustrations. 256 pages.

Making Country-Rustic Furniture. Hundreds of photos, patterns, and detailed scaled drawings reveal construction methods, woodworking techniques, and Spielman's professional secrets for making indoor and outdoor furniture in the distinctly attractive Country-Rustic style. Covered are all aspects of furniture making from choosing the best wood for the job to texturing smooth boards. Among the dozens of projects are mailboxes, cabinets, shelves, coffee tables, weather vanes, doors, panelling, plant stands and many other durable and economical pieces. 400 illustrations. 4 pages in full color. 164 pages.

Making Wood Decoys. A clear step-by-step approach to the basics of decoy carving. This book is abundantly illustrated with closeup photos for designing, selecting, and obtaining woods; tools; feather detailing; painting; and finishing of decorative and working decoys. Six different professional decoy artists are featured. Photo gallery (4 pages in full color) along with numerous detailed plans for various popular decoys. 160 pages.

Making Wood Signs. Designing, selecting woods and tools, and every process through finishing are clearly covered. Hand-carved, power-carved, routed, and sandblasted processes in small to huge signs are presented. Foolproof guides for professional letters and ornaments. Hundreds of photos (4 pages in full color). Lists sources for supplies and special tooling. 144 pages.

Realistic Decoys. Spielman and master carver Keith Bridenhagen reveal their successful techniques for carving, feather-texturing, painting, and finishing wood decoys. Details that you can't find elsewhere—anatomy, attitudes, markings, and the easy step-by-step approach to perfect delicate procedures—make this book invaluable. Includes listings for contests, shows, and sources of tools and supplies. 274 closeup photos, 28 in color. 224 pages.

Router Handbook. With nearly 600 illustrations of every conceivable bit, attachment, jig, and fixture, plus every possible operation, this definitive guide has revolutionized router applications. It begins with safety and maintenance tips, then forges ahead into all aspects of dovetailing, freehanding, advanced duplication, and more. Details for over 50 projects are included. 224 pages.

Router Jigs & Techniques. A practical encyclopedia of information, covering the latest equipment to use with your router, it describes all the newest of commercial routing machines, along with jigs, bits, and other aids and devices. The book not only provides invaluable tips on how to determine the router and bits best suited to your needs, but tells you how to get the most out of your equipment once it is bought. Over 800 photos and illustrations. 384 pages.

Scroll Saw Handbook. This companion volume to *Scroll Saw Pattern Book* covers the essentials of this versatile tool, including the basics (how scroll saws work, blades to use, etc.) and the advantages and disadvantages of the general types and specific brand-name models available on the market. All cutting techniques are detailed, including compound and bevel sawing, making inlays, reliefs, and recesses, cutting metals and other non-woods, and marquetry. There's even a section on transferring patterns to wood! Over 500 illustrations. 256 pages.

Scroll Saw Pattern Book. This companion book to *Scroll Saw Handbook* contains over 450 workable patterns for making wall plaques, refrigerator magnets, candle holders, pegboards, jewelry, ornaments, shelves, brackets, picture frames, signboards, and many more projects. Beginners and experienced scroll saw users alike will find something to intrigue and challenge them. 256 pages.

Scroll Saw Puzzle Patterns. 80 full-size patterns for jigsaw puzzles, standup puzzles and inlay puzzles. With meticulous attention to detail, Patrick and Patricia Spielman provide instruction and step-by-step photos, along with tips on tools and wood selections, for making standup puzzles in the shape of dinosaurs, camels, hippopotamuses, alligators—even a family of elephants! Inlay puzzle patterns include

basic shapes, numbers, an accurate piece-together map of the United States and a host of other colorful educational and enjoyable games for children. 8 pages of color. 256 pages.

Working Green Wood with PEG. Covers every process for making beautiful, inexpensive projects from green wood without cracking, splitting, or warping. Hundreds of clear photos and drawings show every step from obtaining the raw wood through shaping, treating, and finishing your PEG-treated projects. 175 unusual project ideas. Lists supply sources. 160 pages.

Index

alphabets & numerals, 112–113, 121, 127
  Gay Nineties, 102–111
animals
  Cat, 90
  Deer, 88, 94, 100–101
  Dragon, 95–97
  Frog, 89
  Giraffe, 92
  Griffin, 98
  Horse, 93
  Reindeer and sleigh, 210
  Sea horse, 91
  Squirrel, 92
  Unicorns, 99
arches, Victorian, 190–194
architectural brackets, 179–183
arrows, 211

balusters, 184–185
Bird and flowers sign, 136–137
birds, 68–72, 74–78
  Ducks, 79–83
  Hummingbird, 84–85
  Owl and bat, 87
  Roosters, 86
  Stork, 73
brackets, 138–139, 172–178. *See also* shelves
  architectural, 179–183
Butterfly, 34, 74

Candle holder, 36
Card holder, 48–49
Carriage, 220–223
Cat, 90
Chess- or checkerboard, 246–247
Christmas ornaments, 209–210
Circular rose, 245
clocks, 227–237
  German-style wall, 238–244
country designs
  Butterfly, 34
  Heart-shaped wreath, 29
  Lantern, 31

  Pineapple, 30
  Swan, 32–33
  Welcome sign, 35
Cupid silhouette, 14
Deer, 88, 94, 100–101
Desk name-signs, 121
Dragon, 95–97
Ducks, 79–83
enlargement of patterns, 7–8
Explorer, 16th-century, 249
Family supper silhouette, 19, 22–23
Family tree sign, 133–135
Floral inlay or overlay, 206–207
frames. *See* mirror & photo frames
fretwork, 6–7
Frog, 89
gable ornaments, 195–197
Gay Nineties alphabet & numerals, 102–111
  on sign, 114
German-style wall clock, 238–244
Giraffe, 92
Girl-in-swing silhouette, 24–25
Griffin, 98
grilles, 198–202, 249
Hand mirror, 40–41
Heart-shaped
  frame, 55
  inlay or overlay, 203, 205
  wreath, 29
home accessories
  Candle holder, 36
  Card holder, 48–49
  Hand mirror, 40–41
  Key rack, 42
  Letter opener, 37
  Pencil holder, 43–44
  Plant hanger, 38–39
  Sleigh, 50–53
  Wheelbarrow, 45–47
Horn, 65
Horse, 93

For information on how you can have *Better Homes & Gardens*
magazine delivered to your door, write to:
Robert Austin, P.O. Box 4536, Des Moines, IA 50336.

Horse-and-carriage silhouette, 26–27
Hummingbird, 84–85
inlays, 203–208
Key rack, 42
Lantern, 31
Letter opener, 37
Mandala-like, 248
metric equivalency, 250
miniatures, 224–226
mirror & photo frames
    Heart-shaped, 55
    Oval, 54
    Oval with shelf, 62–63
    Rectangular, 56–58, 60–61
    Square, 58–59
    Standing, 64
musical designs
    Horn, 65
    Musical motif, 66–67
    Violin, 65
Nautical silhouettes, 212–215
numerals. *See* alphabets & numerals
Old-fashioned bicyclist silhouette, 17
Old-fashioned touring car, 218–219
Oval floral inlay or overlay, 206
Oval frame, 54
Oval frame with shelf, 62–63
overlays, 203–208
Owl and bat, 87
pantograph, 7
patterns. *See also specific patterns*
    enlargement of, 7–8
    multiple uses for, 12
    reduction of, 7
    transferral of, 8
Pencil holder, 43–44
photo frames. *See* mirror & photo frames
piercing work, 10
Pineapple, 30
Plant hanger, 38–39
Rectangular frame, 56–58, 60–61
reduction of pattern, 7
Reindeer and sleigh, 210
Roosters, 86
Sailboat silhouette, 15
Sea horse, 91
Seated-girl silhouette, 18, 20–21
shelves, 138–159, 162–171
    Snake, 160–161
signs
    alphabets & numerals for, 127

Basic alphabet, 121
Bird and flowers, 136–137
Desk name, 121
Double hearts and arrows, 127–129
Family tree, 133–135
with Gay Nineties lettering, 114
with post, 132
Signboard, 114, 116–119
Simple, 114
Single heart, 120, 122–123
Small desk, 124–125
Wedding bells, 127, 130–131
silhouettes
    Apple, 15
    Cupid, 14
    Family supper, 19, 22–23
    Girl in swing, 24–25
    Horse and carriage, 26–27
    Nautical, 212–215
    Old-fashioned bicyclist, 17
    Sailboat, 15
    Seated girl, 18, 20–21
    Tree, 15
    Unicorn, 16
    Women's portrait, 28
Single-heart sign, 120, 122–123
Sleigh, 50–53
    and Reindeer, 210
Small desk sign, 124–125
Snake shelf, 160–161
Square frame, 58–59
Squirrel, 92
Standing photo frame, 64
starting, basics for, 10–11
Stork, 73
Swan, 32–33
templates, 8
Touring car, 218–219
transferral of pattern, 8
Tree silhouette, 14
trim, 186–189
Unicorns, 16, 99
vehicles, 218–223
Victorian arches, 190–194
Violin, 65
Wedding bells, 127, 130–131
Welcome sign, 35
Wheelbarrow, 45–47
Wheels, 216–217
Women's portrait silhouette, 28
wood materials, 8–9
Wreath, heart-shaped, 29